LEADING OUR CHILDREN TO GOD

LEADING OUR CHILDREN TO GOD

A FAITH GUIDE FOR CATHOLIC PARENTS

William R. Brinkmann
William T. Ditewig

AVE MARIA PRESS
NOTRE DAME, INDIANA 46556

Permissions:

Scripture texts are taken from *The Jerusalem Bible,* copyright © 1966 by Darton, Longman & Todd, Ltd. and Doubleday & Company, Inc. Reprinted by permission of the publisher.

Excerpts from *Sharing the Light of Faith,* National Catechetical Directory for Catholics of the United States, copyright © 1979, by the United States Catholic Conference, Department of Education, Washington, D.C., are used by permission of the copyright owner. All rights reserved.

Excerpts from Vatican II documents are taken from *Vatican Council II:* The Conciliar and Post Conciliar Documents, copyright © 1975 by Costello Publishing Company, Inc., and Reverend Austin Flannery, O.P. Used with permission.

Nihil Obstat:

Rev. Bartholomew J. O'Leary
Censor Librorum

Imprimatur:

Joseph A. Ferrario
Bishop of Honolulu

International Standard Book Number: 0-87793-310-3

Library of Congress Catalog Card Number: 83-72992

Cover design: Katherine A. Robinson

Photography:

John David Arms, 32; C. W. Brookins, 5; Paul Buddle, 45, 52, 80; Rohn Engh, cover, 3; Jim Frier, 74-75; H. T. Kellner, 26-27; Jean-Claude Lejeune, 36-37; Robert Maust, 19; Carolyn Mckeone, 42; Joanne Meldrum, 56, 68; James L. Shaffer, 57; Vernon Sigl, 94-95; Bob Taylor, 14, 23, 60, 92; Kenneth Tighe, 8-9; Paul Tucker, 86; Jim Whitmer, 15.

Printed and bound in the United States of America.

CONTENTS

William Brinkmann
and
William Ditewig
are both career naval officers who have been active in religious education programs in numerous parish communities as teachers and coordinators, and share a deep concern for the continuous religious education of fellow parents and their children.

Brinkmann, a graduate of St. Louis University, holds a master's degree from the University of Southern California and has taught on the high school and college level. Ditewig is a graduate of St. Ambrose College and holds a master's degree from Pepperdine University.

To Our Parents

INTRODUCTION

Dear Fellow Parents,

We have written this book for you, the Catholic parent. We are both husbands and fathers who are concerned with transmitting the joy and peace of Christ in our own families. As educators, we want to extend the message to others, especially to those with whom we have most in common: other parents.

In this book, you will find a review of the essential elements of our Catholic Christian faith. The book also shares some of our own family experiences in the form of teachable moments and actual events. Teachable moments are those times when children show interest and have requested information about our faith. These experiences have been given in the hope that they may illustrate our faith in daily life.

The church teaches that parents are the primary educators of their children in faith. But many parents don't feel qualified to perform this function. In our experience as religious education teachers, we have met many parents who rely solely on the CCD or parish school to pass on the beliefs and values of our faith. While one of the roles of the church is to educate, that does not and cannot relieve us of our own responsibilities for Christian growth within our families.

You see, Christianity is a faith based not just on what we know, but also on what we feel and who we are. While a formal school can help with intellectual growth, the truly Christian family is the best place for us to share and grow in the moral dimensions of our faith. Children can learn the Apostles' Creed in school, but they will grow in the beliefs espoused in the Creed when they see the faith lived at home.

VATICAN II

"As it is the parents who have given life to their children, on them lies the gravest obligation of educating their family. They must therefore be recognized as being primarily and principally responsible for their education. The role of parents in education is of such importance that it is almost impossible to provide an adequate substitute. It is therefore the duty of parents to create a family atmosphere inspired by love and devotion to God and their fellow-men which will promote an integrated, personal and social education of their children" (Declaration on Christian Education, No. 3).

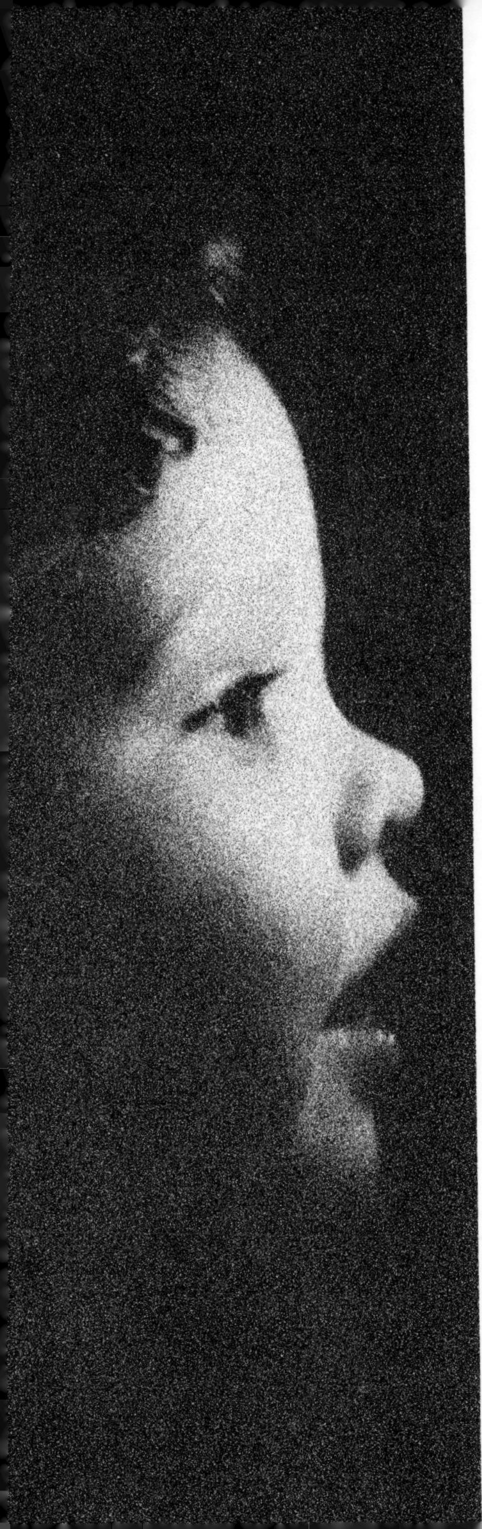

The message of God is clear and simple. God loves each of us, and he wants each of us to love him. He loves us so much that he sent his own Son to bring us back to him. God calls out to us, and our answer is an active, loving faith.

We have drawn on four major resources in various ways, and we will be sharing them with you as we go along. First is the bible. Most of us have neglected the bible as a source of personal contact with the Word of God. We will draw on scripture to show you the written foundation of our very essence as Christians.

A second resource is the collection of documents from the Second Vatican Council. Without changing the solid keel of our faith, the Council Fathers hoisted fresh sails and set a new course for the church, one which is close to the course set by Christ himself.

Our third resource is a book entitled *Sharing the Light of Faith,* the National Catechetical Directory (NCD) for Catholics of the United States. In this volume, published in 1979, the American bishops organized principles and guidelines for spiritual formation. The NCD is an expression of a vital, growing and loving faith-community, with an emphasis on practical application of faith rather than on theological dissertations.

But our most important resource was our families. We have seen how important God's love has been in our own homes. We will share some of these times with you, knowing that each of you will see the similarities to your own experience.

We hope this book will be as useful to you who read it as it has been for us who wrote it.

In Christ,
William Brinkmann
William Ditewig

PROLOGUE

God's Story

Once, long, long ago, there was nothing, and no one, except me.

Imagine a world with no TV, no cars, no stereos.

Imagine a world with no dogs, no birds, no goldfish.

Imagine a world with no mountains, no oceans, no valleys.

Imagine a world with no sun, no moon, no stars.

Imagine a world with no people.

Imagine no world.

But, even then, I was—alone.

I wanted to share my life, so I created time and space, and lit the sky above with my stars. I created earth, water, fire and air. I created animals, plants and flowers.

All of these things were good. But they were not enough.

I wanted someone to tend all that I had made: someone like me. So, I created you. I gave you some of my own life and you became a part of me. For this reason I could talk with you and share myself with you. I explained all that I had done, and what I expected you to do. We were very happy, you and I.

But then you began tending my creations only for yourselves. You forgot that I had given you everything.

You forgot me!

I tried again and again to draw you back to me. I sent special messengers. I showed you strange and awesome wonders. Some of you came back, but most did not.

I knew then that I would have to go among you as one of you to show just how much I love you. So I came and lived with you. I told you that I was love itself and that to live forever you must love me and one another.

Many understood my message and returned to me. Others wanted to, but did not have the faith or the courage. And others in great fear rose up against me, made fun of me, imprisoned me, nailed me to a tree, and killed me!

But even in the face of such fear and hatred, I did not forget you: In the fullness of my life and love, I rose from death and restored your life. I will never leave you, for you are my people and I am your God!

LISTEN TO ME, MY PEOPLE!

You are my special love. I want you to care for one another and for all I have made. As I have given you life, I will give you all you need. Don't worry about anything else. After all, I have shown you life, death and rebirth.

Love me, my people, and we will live together happily ever after.

I

THE FATHER REVEALS HIMSELF

In "God's Story" we read that God cares for us and shares himself with us. God's part in this is known as revelation; our response to God is an active faith.

The fact that we can enjoy a deeply personal and dynamic relationship with God is the basis for our Catholic faith.

There are two things we should remember about revelation:

1. *Revelation is a free gift from God:* We are not entitled to it; we did not earn it. God decides when, where, how and to whom he will reveal himself.

2. *Revelation is a call to action:* St. John put it this way in his first letter:

Anyone who says, "I know him,"
and does not keep his commandments,
is a liar,
refusing to admit the truth (1 Jn 2:4).

So revelation is not something that we can accept passively. It is not water poured into an empty glass. Through revelation, God is initiating a *dia*logue, not a *mono*logue: He expects and invites an active response.

The fact that God reveals himself to people really impresses children. It is such a normal activity and gives us something in common with the people in the bible.

NCD

"The history of salvation is the story of God's entry into human affairs to save human beings from sin and bring them to Himself" (No. 83).

VATICAN II

"It pleased God, in his goodness and wisdom, to reveal himself and to make known the mystery of his will (cf. Eph. 1:9). His will was that men should have access to the Father, through Christ, the Word made flesh, in the Holy Spirit, and thus become sharers in the divine nature (cf. Eph. 2:18; 2 Pet. 1:4). By this revelation, then, the invisible God (cf. Col. 1:15, 1 Tim. 1:17), from the fullness of his love, addresses men as his friends (cf. Ex. 33:11; Jn. 15; 14-15), and moves among them (cf. Bar. 3:38), in order to invite and receive them into his own company" (Dogmatic Constitution on Divine Revelation, No. 2).

SCRIPTURE

"Yahweh would speak with Moses face to face, as a man speaks with his friend" (Ex 33:11).

"You are my friends,
if you do what I command you.
I shall not call you servants any more,
because a servant does not know
his master's business;
I call you friends,
because I have made known to you
everything I have learnt from my Father" (Jn 15:14-15).

GOD DOESN'T TALK

While putting the children to bed one evening I said good night for what I hoped would be the last time. And Amy said: "God doesn't talk to me."

"What do you mean?"

"You know, like when God told Abraham what to do, or like that man in the movie, *Oh God!*"

"Where do we find out about God talking to people?"

"In the bible."

"I think reading the bible is like God talking to us, because I think he'd say lots of the same things to us that he said to the people in the bible."

"OK, but I still keep waiting for a whisper like Father Jack talked about." This was a reference to a recent sermon on God speaking to us in little things.

"That would be great, wouldn't it? Sometimes when I'm praying for help with a hard problem, I just keep quiet. Then, after a while, the answer becomes very clear."

"That's your con—, con—,"

"Conscience," I helped. "Maybe conscience is a way God speaks to us. The other day at work we saw a rainbow from our window. It was beautiful. I think God was showing us his beauty. Are there any other ways he talks to us?"

"Well, like when Father Jack is talking, he is talking sort of for God."

"Sure is. Any other ways?"

"Well, he gave Jesus to us."

"Right, and that shows us how much he loves us, doesn't it? Let's count the ways God talks to us: in the bible, through prayer, in helping us with problems, in his creation, through his ministers and priests, and especially through Jesus. So he really does talk to us, doesn't he?"

"But, Dad."

"Yes?"

"I'm still going to wait for him to whisper."

"Good night, Amy."

"Good night, Daddy."

We Catholics believe that God reveals himself to us through the bible and tradition. We'll look at tradition as a source of revelation when we talk about the church later on; right now, though, let's look at God's written word to us: the bible.

The Bible: God's Library

It is far beyond the scope of this book to get into any fine points of biblical scholarship. But if we expect to use the bible as a source of comfort, inspiration and revelation we need to know something about it. After all, the bible is for all of us, not just for biblical scholars. Let's face it, though, when most of us were growing up very little attention was paid to educating us about the bible. As a result, many of us find ourselves facing adult problems and responsibilities without an adult appreciation of what the bible is, what it tells us, or even how to use it.

In November 1965, the Second Vatican Council declared that all the faithful should have easy access to the scriptures and that they should "learn by frequent

reading of the divine Scriptures. . . ." The Council Fathers even quoted St. Jerome to drive their point home: "Ignorance of the Scriptures is ignorance of Christ."

Let's take a look at ten basic questions about the bible.

1. What is scripture?

Sacred Scripture—the bible—is really a collection of 73 small books. The Greek word for little books is *biblia*, from which we get our English word bible.

2. How are the books of the bible organized?

The books of the bible are divided into two parts:

Old Testament, which reveals God's relationship with the ancient Jews and sets forth God's plan for salvation of all people; and the

New Testament, which reveals the fullness of God's goodness in the person, life, death and resurrection of Jesus Christ.

3. Are the books alike?

No, just about all literary styles can be found in the bible: Poetry, law, history, songs and stories are all there.

4. In what language was the bible written?

Most of the Old Testament was written in Hebrew, while the New Testament was written in Greek and Aramaic. The first translations were made into Greek (this version is known as the *Septuagint*), from which a Latin translation was made by St. Jerome (this one was called the *Vulgate*). The first English translations were then made from the Latin version. All these translations from translations caused serious problems for scholars since exact literal translations from one language to another are impossible, and some meaning was distorted. Fortunately, the last 25 years or so have seen translators use original texts as their source, and recent discoveries of more original texts have provided them with nearly a complete set of ancient manuscripts. Not only are today's translations closer in spirit to the originals, they are expressed in contemporary English, making them more understandable.

5. What is meant when we say the bible is inspired?

In short, we say a biblical book is inspired because we believe that God is revealed in it and that he is the origin of that revelation.

6. Who decides whether or not a book is inspired?

The church determines if a book is inspired. Inspiration cannot be determined by any study of the external characteristics of the book itself; we believe that inspiration is determined by God's revelation through Catholic tradition.

7. What is the canon of the bible?

The canon is a list of all the books recognized by the church as inspired by God. Although Catholics and Protestants believe in the same New Testament, they differ on seven books in the Old Testament. These seven books, which Protestants do not believe are inspired, are called deuterocanonical.

8. Since we believe the bible is divinely inspired, does that mean that everything in it is literally and historically accurate?

No! The authors did not write these books as we would write a modern history book. When we think of history, we think of dates, places and people. The writers of the bible were concerned only with God and his actions. This is known as "salvation history." The bible is God's story, not man's. So, for example, when the creation accounts were written in Genesis, they were not meant to explain how God did it, but rather to

NCD

"What we are to believe is found in tradition and scripture, which together 'form one sacred deposit of the word of God which is committed to the Church' " (No. 59, contained quotation from Dogmatic Constitution on Divine Revelation, No. 10).

VATICAN II

"Sacred Tradition and sacred Scripture, then, are bound closely together, and communicate one with the other. For both of them, flowing out of the same divine well-spring, come together in some fashion to form one thing, and move towards the same goal. Sacred Scripture is the speech of God as it is put down in writing under the breath of the Holy Spirit. And Tradition transmits in its entirety the Word of God which has been entrusted to the apostles by Christ the Lord and the Holy Spirit" (Dogmatic Constitution on Divine Revelation, No. 9).

convey the awesome fact that the all-powerful and loving God of the Jews had created the universe, and that it was not the act of some pagan god or an accident of nature.

The bible is not, and was never supposed to be, scientific. The Jews were telling the world that their God was more powerful than any other force in the universe, that this God was responsible for everything in the universe, including creation, and that this God lives and loves all people. This is what salvation history is all about. Inspiration means that revelation is contained in the writing; it does *not* mean that every individual word is a revelation.

9. Do all the books have a unifying theme?

All of the books of the bible deal with God's relationship with humankind. Specifically, they relate God's master plan of creation and salvation. An essential element of this plan is contained in what is known as God's covenant with his people. Each book of the bible deals in one way or another with this covenant.

10. What exactly is a covenant?

Since we are incapable of comprehending the divine, God reveals himself in human terms and expressions. God is like a good teacher who makes the most complicated subjects meaningful by using the students' experiences and abilities rather than his or her own. So when God began his relationship with the Jews, he used ideas and concepts familiar to them. One of these concepts was the ancient idea of a covenant—an agreement.

The early Jews were essentially nomads surrounded by powerful and politically adept neighbors. To survive as a people, they came to rely on formal contracts to settle disputes within their own communities

SCRIPTURE

"And to some, his gift was that they should be apostles; to some, prophets; to some, evangelists; to some, pastors and teachers; so that the saints together make a unity in the work of service, building up the body of Christ. In this way we are all to come to unity in our faith and in our knowledge of the Son of God, until we become the perfect Man, fully mature with the fullness of Christ himself" (Eph 4:11-13).

and to establish productive relations with their neighbors. A covenant was a type of contract common in ancient and medieval times. In this type, a lord or king and his subjects formed an alliance in which the subjects swore obedience and allegiance to the king. In return, the lord, although not legally bound in our modern sense, agreed to protect his people and provide for their welfare.

God's covenant with man expands on this type of human contract. The covenant is simply this: "They shall be my people and I will be their God" (Ez 11:20). The key difference in this covenant is that God and his people are bound not by legal sanctions but by dedicated love. God's love for his people will never wane, even when the people forget him. God's call to each of us is to share in this covenant, as renewed and perfected by Christ. The covenant is the very basis of our salvation. Christ came to renew and rededicate God's covenant with all people.

Read your bible

These questions and answers barely scratch the surface of what is to be found in the bible. The best way to learn about it is to read it. You can't learn how to swim or paint or ride a bike by listening to someone else talk about these things. The same principle applies to the word of God.

And please remember that the bible was written from God to you and your family. Would you leave a letter from a loved one unopened and unread? The bible is just that: a love letter from God. Open it!

The God of Our Fathers

Now that we've looked at how God has revealed himself to us, let's look at what God has shown us about

NCD

"The Bible is not just a book to be read and studied. It contains God's word, which should be the object of our prayerful meditation. As a source of inspiration and spiritual nourishment, the Bible ought to be a constant companion. . . . The books of the New Testament, especially the Gospels, enjoy pre-eminence as principal witness of the life and teachings of Jesus, the Incarnate Word" (No. 60).

himself. Who is God, based on what he has told us in scripture? How did this relationship between God and his people begin? What does God expect us to do? What does God look like?

Our image of God is based on the human terms of the bible, which meant certain things to the ancient Israelite. The same expressions, filtered through today's cultures and values, sometimes lose their original punch. We need to be able to read scripture intelligently and with sensitivity to the divine realities and religious truths it contains.

Like us, our children develop a picture of God which is taken from their culture. This picture and indeed God himself are very real to them. Talking about what God might look like has helped our children learn what God is.

I SAW GOD TODAY

When our daughter said that she saw God, my wife asked: "Where?"

"At the library."

"What did he look like?"

"He was old and had white hair."

"So you saw a picture of someone's idea of God."

"Yeah, in a book, but it was God. How would you draw God?"

"I think I'd draw something powerful, and refreshing and invisible, something like the wind."

"I really like that."

"It's not original."

"I still like it."

Much of what we first learn about God is based on what he has revealed to us through his relationship with the ancient Jews. The authors of the books of the bible were Jewish people who had experienced God in a special way and were called to share their experience with others. To better understand God, we need to understand more about the Jews and their role in God's story.

All the peoples of the ancient Middle East lived lives closely entwined with nature. Those people who specialized in commerce relied on the wind to carry their goods from port to port. Farming communities needed favorable weather for a bounteous harvest to sustain their own communities and for trade with others. Ranchers and shepherds were concerned with those conditions which would promote healthy and fertile stock.

As might be expected of people who lived so intimately with nature, they became experts on its cycles and realities. Those of us today who work in offices or factories take for granted our ability to work most of the time regardless of the weather. But think about it a bit. If you were part of a caravan trying to make its way through the desert, the last thing you would need or want would be a windstorm. On the other hand, if you were a Phoenician sailor trying to get goods to Cyprus, you would welcome a brisk wind rather than a becalmed sea. In relating to nature, many Middle Eastern people began seeing personality traits in its elements. The power of the wind was actually seen as a person, as was the sun, fire, rain and so on.

In fact, since these personalities were so vital to the survival of the community, they soon became revered by the people as gods, beings who were responsible for the course of nature. Although these nature

gods were powerful in the eyes of their worshipers, they were limited as well. They could be ruled by emotions such as jealousy, hate, anger and rivalry. They could be driven by sexual impulses. Some even had to eat, drink and breathe in order to survive. Since these gods were limited, the people believed they could appease and even manipulate them if they followed set rituals which seemed to work in the past. The rituals became complex, and a special group was set up within the community to keep track of them. These "priests" were little more than what we would call magicians today. They memorized their lines and actions to make the gods give rain, a good harvest, gentle seas, or whatever else was wanted.

This was the religious environment which surrounded the ancient Jews. Why didn't they believe as their neighbors did? What made them so different? Were they great scholars? They were not a great military nation like Rome or Egypt. They were not great philosophers like the Greeks. They were a simple, earthy, realistic people who had to spend most of their time and energy just staying alive. In short, nothing from a human perspective made the Jews a remarkable people. But, suddenly, God thrust himself into their midst as he chose them to receive his revelation, an action which would change the whole course of human existence. The Old Testament is the written expression of that great revelation.

Let's take a look at just three of the many things which are revealed to us through the pages of the Old Testament.

1. The God of the Jews is no imitation: He is the one powerful Lord over all the universe, not one of the petty nature gods of the pagans. Even the Hebrew words used in referring to God are based on concepts of power. He is so powerful that he alone is responsible for the very act of creation itself. The bible says all this repeatedly and beautifully. Here are just a few examples:

> I am Yahweh, unrivalled;
> there is no other God besides me (Is 45:5).
>
> God said to Moses, "I Am who I Am. This," he added, "is what you must say to the sons of Israel: 'I Am has sent me to you' " (Ex 3:14).
>
> "Listen, Israel: Yahweh our God is the one Yahweh. You shall love Yahweh your God with all your heart, with all your soul, with all your strength" (Dt 6:4-5).
>
> Thus says Israel's king
> and his redeemer, Yahweh Sabaoth:
> I am the first and the last;
> there is no other God besides me (Is 44:6).

And this striking passage from Isaiah which says it all:

> Thus says God, Yahweh,
> he who created the heavens and spread them out,
> who gave shape to the earth and what comes from it,
> who gave breath to its people
> and life to the creatures that move in it:
>
> I, Yahweh, have called you to serve the cause of right;
> I have taken you by the hand and formed you;
> I have appointed you as covenant of the people and light of the nations,
>
> to open the eyes of the blind,
> to free captives from prison,
> and those who live in darkness from the dungeon.
>
> My name is Yahweh,
> I will not yield my glory to another,
> nor my honor to idols.

VATICAN II

"In the sacred books the Father who is in heaven comes lovingly to meet his children, and talks to them" (Dogmatic Constitution on Divine Revelation, No. 21).

"Let them remember, however, that prayer should accompany the reading of sacred Scripture, so that a dialogue takes place between God and man. For, 'we speak to him when we pray; we listen to him when we read the divine oracles' " (Dogmatic Constitution on Divine Revelation, No. 25).

SCRIPTURE

"The word of God is something alive and active: it cuts like any double-edged sword but more finely" (Heb 4:12).

"And now I commend you to God, and to the word of his grace that has power to build you up and to give you your inheritance among all the sanctified" (Acts 20:32).

See how former predictions have come true.
Fresh things I now foretell;
before they appear I tell you of them (Is 42:5-9).

2. God loves his people so much that he has entered into a covenant of love with them:

For his love is strong,
his faithfulness eternal (Ps 117:2).

He takes our sins farther away
than the east is from the west.

As tenderly as a father treats his children (Ps 103:12-13).

I will give them a single heart and I will put a new spirit in them. . . . Then they shall be my people and I will be their God (Ez 11:19-20).

3. People have trouble living up to their part of the covenant, and God promises to send them a savior, someone who will restore God's life in them and make the covenant whole again:

And say to all faint hearts,
"Courage! Do not be afraid.

"Look, your God is coming,
vengeance is coming,
the retribution of God;
he is coming to save you" (Is 35:4).

The Teachable Moment

So what does all this mean to us and our families? Actually, children raised on superheroes and the "force" of *Star Wars* find it easy, natural and satisfying to accept God as an all-powerful being who looks out for their welfare. As indicated in the stories already related in this chapter, there are special moments of curiosity or excitement that we can use to relate God's loving power to family life. At dinner time, we discuss the day's events and relate them to God's providence. And, as a family we have experienced God in nature. Discussing family happenings in terms of experiencing God has made our relationship with God very real.

Educators are fond of exhorting us to capitalize on "the teachable moment." This means we should use these special opportunities to do our teaching because interest is high and information has been requested. By responding to inquiries, we are providing thoughts and information which trigger new questions and new answers, and we are feeding a genuine interest.

We would like to share some of our teachable moments with you. Rest assured, most of these occasions were not seen as teachable moments while we were living them. Many of them happened while we were preoccupied with something else and not really in the mood to relate the experience to God and his call. But, after some reflection, it became obvious that it sometimes was for this very reason that they become such great teachable moments.

Anything which offers a common goal, planning as family, and a sense of adventure or accomplishment—camping, hiking, picnicking, sailing, working together—helps bring families closer. However, there is another significant advantage which these activities provide to the parent who is involved with his children's spiritual development. Outings in nature provide a wealth of images, sensations and experiences which are food for later discussions. A large portion of the teachings (parables, proverbs, images, comparisons) of the bible are based on nature. The power of wind, the abundance of life, the cleansing of water, God's providence for wildlife, were made real for our children during hiking trips. Climbing the side of a steep hill gives significance to the statement, "The Lord is my staff."

TAKING A HIKE

While hiking in a national park in Hawaii, we were making our way through a lava flow which had covered the area several years before. The power of the destructive force of the volcano and its molten lava was very impressive, but the children were equally taken by the fact that in remote crevices of the lava small plants had begun to grow. New life was emerging; God was renewing the earth. We discussed the fact that God is continually renewing his creation and similarly renewing his spirit in us. Regardless of the devastation we might meet in life, renewal and rebirth await us in our relationship with God.

Sometimes we think of God as we see him reflected in nature. But it is important to remember that nature, no matter how powerful, is not God, and that we can and must turn to God for help.

HER NAME WAS PAMELA

Pamela was born in May 1976 near the small South Pacific islands of the Truk Lagoon. She began life quietly enough, but as she grew and got stronger she became restless and ruthless. Soon, she had grown so powerful that she destroyed everything she touched. She was a typhoon.

My family would meet Pamela face to face. I had been stationed with the Navy on Guam for a year and a half. In that time, several tropical

storms and typhoons had threatened Guam, but none had hit the island directly in five years. Pamela was going to be different.

May 18 dawned bright and clear. It was a big day at home. Tom was celebrating his fourth birthday. Steve would celebrate his second birthday just four days later. How different those two days would be! At work we were informed that Pamela was going to pass near Guam. By 2:50 that afternoon, Typhoon Condition III (48-hour warning) was set. We all thought the forecasters were nuts—the weather was great, not even a cloud in the sky.

Our birthday party for Tom went off without even a passing thought to Pamela. It just seemed like all the other times when storms were predicted and then passed us by. We couldn't have been less concerned.

At 10:44 p.m. all Navy ships were ordered out of port.

At 9:30 a.m. on May 19, Typhoon Condition II (24-hour warning) was set. Pamela was now forecast to pass 200 miles south of us. Whenever we had gone into Condition II before, the weather had been predictably rainy and windy. By 6:00 p.m., it still wasn't raining; in fact, we enjoyed a beautiful Pacific sunset: warm, glowing colors and soft, caressing breezes.

Overnight, things changed. It was raining steadily now and the winds were gusting over 40 mph. At 9:30 a.m. on the 20th, Typhoon Condition I (12-hour warning) was set. Pamela had turned toward Guam and was now forecast to pass only 30 miles away. Not only that, Pamela was reaching her prime. A tropical storm is

classified a typhoon when winds exceed 74 mph. A typhoon is reclassified a supertyphoon when those winds double and exceed 150 miles per hour. Pamela now had winds gusting to 185 miles per hour.

At 5:05 p.m., Supertyphoon Pamela struck.

How can we describe such an experience to those who have not encountered something like it? The constant, screaming noise, like a howling spirit, from which there is no refuge. The extreme, nearly instantaneous changes in air pressure which ripped into our ears until they ached. The sweet smell of earth and water being whipped into a frenzy until all these things—the noise, the wind, the rain—become a palpable, tangible and living thing.

The impact of such an experience on me personally and on my family is hard to calculate. My wife, who goes into nervous fits before a dinner party at home, was the source of great strength and calm throughout the uproar. Steve, our two-year-old, was scared, but with the beautiful, trusting innocence of a baby, remained relatively calm. Four-year-old Tom, a little older and more "experienced" than his brother, knew whatever was happening was far out of the ordinary. Never claustrophobic before, he screamed much of the time, running from door to door in the house trying in vain to "get outa here!"

For my part, I was a kindred spirit with Tom. When the storm started, I felt confident that we would be able to protect ourselves from it, while enjoying a sort of family camp-out in our little shelter beneath the stairs. But, when the wind and rain battered away our living room and second-floor windows, I began to see that I was not in control after all. As the storm intensified, we were flooded out of our shelter and were forced to retreat to our lanai, a sort of enclosed patio. The lanai had been added on to our house and was not typhoon-proof, but it was the driest part of our house at the time.

Up to this point, I was treating Pamela as a god. When nothing I did was good enough to appease her, I panicked and despaired. But then, finally, as we huddled on a couch in our now flooded lanai, I remembered how to pray to the only one who really matters:

> Lord, I beg you, keep us safe.
> Let us see the sun again.
> Help me to know how I can protect my family from this fury.

We survived. Later, during the recovery operations, we learned that our lanai was the only one in our neighborhood not severely damaged or blown away. The Lord had preserved us.

The experience of the typhoon is a part of our family lore now, and has provided teachable moments for us to discuss God's providence. We have learned from it that even after such an experience of God, his nature still exceeds our understanding.

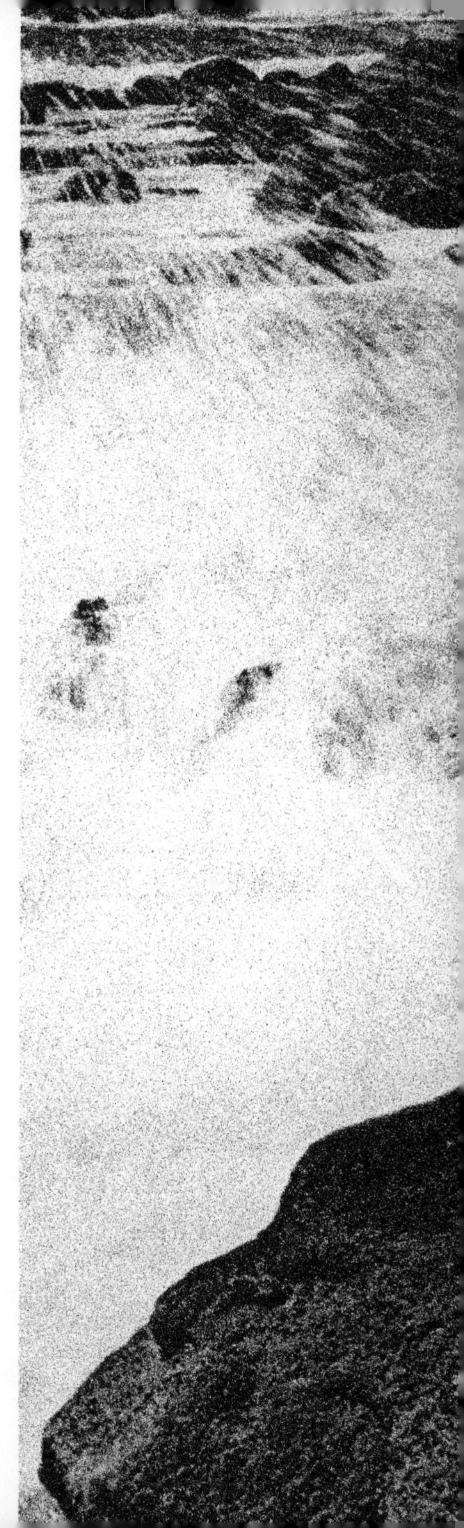

WHO MADE GOD

Often when discussing the nature of God with our children we run into the mystery of God. Amy once said, "What bothers me is, who made God?"

Russ replied, "Amy, nobody made God. He always was!"

"Oh, I know that, but I mean before all that, who made him?"

"Amy, he always was!"

"Was what?"

"Was here!"

I tried to inject that it was hard to understand that there was no time when there was no God.

This conversation reminds us of a very important fact: The nature of God is a mystery. And this is precisely where our response of faith to God's revelation comes in. The Jews knew this and responded with a childlike faith in God's loving and saving activity in their lives. And this is what we must help our children realize: Our God is always there, active in every aspect of our lives. He shares our hopes, joys, tragedies and triumphs. As faithful believers, we accept God's mystery. "Happy are those who have not seen and yet believe" (Jn 20:29).

II

GOD SENDS HIS SON

> See, the days are coming—it is Yahweh who speaks—when I will make a new covenant with the House of Israel (and the House of Judah), but not a covenant like the one I made with their ancestors on the day I took them by the hand to bring them out of the land of Egypt. They broke that covenant of mine, so I had to show them who was master. It is Yahweh who speaks. No, this is the covenant I will make with the House of Israel when those days arrive—it is Yahweh who speaks. Deep within them I will plant my Law, writing it on their hearts. Then I will be their God and they shall be my people. There will be no further need for neighbor to try to teach neighbor, or brother to say to brother, "Learn to know Yahweh!" No, they will all know me, the least no less than the greatest—it is Yahweh who speaks—since I will forgive their iniquity and never call their sin to mind (Jer 31:31-34).

In Christ, God's master plan of creation and salvation is brought to perfection. Jesus is our own personal savior, and the savior to a people. He fulfills Jeremiah's prophecy: He writes God's law of love in each of our hearts.

Jesus, God and Man

Jesus is both human and divine. As God, he extends a loving hand to humanity; as a human being, he is the perfect model of response to that love. Over the years, some people have taught that Jesus was more

NCD

"In taking on human flesh through the ever-virgin Mary and entering human history, God's Son, Jesus Christ, renewed the world from within and became for it an abiding source of supernatural life and salvation from sin" (No. 87).

"Jesus Christ is truly divine, God's only begotten Son (cf. Jn 1,18): 'God from God, light from light, true God begotten not made, of one substance with the Father.' (Nicene Creed).

"Jesus is also truly human. As such, He thinks with a human mind, acts with a human will, loves with a human heart. He was made truly one of us, like us in all things except sin" (No. 89).

God than man, while others have said that he was more man than God. Both of these views were condemned early in our church's history. The church teaches that Jesus is completely human "in all things save sin," and he is also completely divine.

Jesus—The Suffering Servant

Once again, the bible is our best source of information about Jesus. The Second Vatican Council teaches that the gospels "faithfully hand on what Jesus Christ, while living among men, really did and taught for their eternal salvation." One of the key passages concerning the nature of Jesus is the famous scene of Peter's confession:

> When Jesus came to the region of Caesarea Philippi he put this question to his disciples, "Who do people say the Son of Man is?" And they said, "Some say he is John the Baptist, some Elijah, and others Jeremiah or one of the prophets." "But you," he said "who do you say I am?" Then Simon Peter spoke up, "You are the Christ," he said "the Son of the living God." Jesus replied, "Simon son of Jonah, you are a happy man! Because it was not flesh and blood that revealed this to you but my Father in heaven" (Mt 16:13-17).
>
> He gave them strict orders not to tell anyone anything about this.
>
> "The Son of Man" he said "is destined to suffer grievously, to be rejected by the elders and chief priests and scribes and to be put to death, and to be raised up on the third day" (Lk 9:21-22).

The title messiah meant something very specific to the Jewish people. It referred to the anointed descendant of King David who would free the people from

VATICAN II

"He who is the 'image of the invisible God' (Col. 1:15), is himself the perfect man who has restored in the children of Adam that likeness to God which had been disfigured ever since the first sin. Human nature, by the very fact that it was assumed, not absorbed, in him, has been raised in us also to a dignity beyond compare. For, by his incarnation, he, the Son of God, has in a certain way united himself with each man" (Pastoral Constitution on the Church in the Modern World, No. 22).

SCRIPTURE

"Just as all men die in Adam, so all men will be brought to life in Christ" (1 Cor 15:22).

"For of all the names in the world given to men, this is the only one by which we can be saved" (Acts 4:12).

"For it is not as if we had a high priest who was incapable of feeling our weaknesses with us; but we have one who has been tempted in every way that we are, though he is without sin" (Heb 4:15).

their political bondage and restore the glorious kingship of David.

Jesus is the messiah but he tells the apostles not to tell anyone because the people would not understand the *true nature of the kingdom.* He broadens and redefines messiah and it is only after his suffering, death and resurrection that the new meaning of messiah comes clear.

The fact that Jesus had to suffer was hard for the apostles to accept. Peter, just moments after Christ blesses him for recognizing him as the messiah, is severely reprimanded for arguing with him about his coming passion and death: "Get behind me, Satan! Because the way you think is not God's way but man's" (Mk 8:33).

Jesus' suffering for our salvation is no less difficult for us to accept than it was for the apostles. It is particularly confusing for kids. Once my son came to me and asked, "Why did Jesus have to die on the cross?" I answered that he did it to show us how much he loved us.

"But he was God," he replied. "Why couldn't he just have told us?"

"Well, God tried for a long time to tell the people how much he loved them. But after a while, they'd forget."

He told me that he still didn't like the idea of Jesus being crucified. It made him feel uneasy that he went to such lengths to save us. He said, "I want to give something back to Jesus, to show him I love him."

I tried to explain to him that we can do just that when we show our love for one another as Jesus taught us. He accepted my answer, but it was clear that the specter of Jesus on the cross was one which would always upset him. Had he been a little older, I might

have pointed out that Christ expects us to suffer with him, so that we will also rise with him:

> "If anyone wants to be a follower of mine, let him renounce himself and take up his cross every day and follow me. For anyone who wants to save his life will lose it; but anyone who loses his life for my sake, that man will save it" (Lk 9:23-25).

Christ's Message

Christ's message is clear: We must put God first in our lives. God has given us everything we have and everything we are. God and the love of God must become our priorities. Since we are the children of God who look to him for everything, we must accept this message with the trusting innocence of children. When the apostles were discussing who among them was the most important, Jesus called over a child, put his arms around the child and said:

> "Anyone who welcomes one of these little children in my name, welcomes me; and anyone who welcomes me welcomes not me but the one who sent me" (Mk 9:37).

In another place, he said:

> "I tell you solemnly, anyone who does not welcome the kingdom of God like a little child will never enter it" (Mk 10:15).

This total acceptance of God's primacy is best lived out by a firm dedication to the great commandment:

> "*You must love the Lord your God with all your heart, with all your soul,* and with all your mind. This is the greatest and the first commandment. The second resembles it: *You must love your neighbor as yourself*" (Mt 22:37-39).

Christ teaches that love of God and love of neighbor spring from the same Spirit and are inseparable.

> Anyone who says, "I love God,"
> and hates his brother,
> is a liar,
> since a man who does not love the brother that he can see
> cannot love God, whom he has never seen (1 Jn 4:20).

We are to love all human beings, even enemies, as we love ourselves; even more, we are to obey Christ's new command to love all others as he has loved us.

> By this command Christ tells us something new—about God, about love, and about ourselves. His commandment to love is new not simply because of the scope and unselfishness of the love involved, but because it summons human beings to love with a divine love called charity, as the Father, Son, and Spirit do. This call carries with it the inner gift of their life and the power of their love, for Christ does not command what is impossible (*NCD*, No. 91).

SCRIPTURE

"I give you a new commandment:
love one another;
just as I have loved you
you also must love one another"
(Jn 13:34).

"This is my commandment:
love one another,
as I have loved you" (Jn 15:12).

The Resurrection: Victory of Love Over Sin

We must constantly remember that it is precisely the fullness of Christ's humanity that makes his resurrection the powerful act it is. Since he was completely human, Christ is really our brother, as well as our God. We are promised the same resurrection. St. Paul tells us that our attitude must be that of Christ:

> His state was divine,
> yet he did not cling
> to his equality with God
> but emptied himself
> to assume the condition of a slave,
> and became as men are;
> and being as all men are,
> he was humbler yet,
> even to accepting death,
> death on a cross.
> But God raised him high
> and gave him the name
> which is above all other names
> so that *all beings*
> in the heavens, on earth and in the underworld,
> *should bend the knee* at the name of Jesus
> and that every tongue should acclaim
> Jesus Christ as Lord,
> to the glory of God the Father (Phil 2:6-11).

The great power of God's love for us is never so awesome or so apparent as it is in Christ's resurrection. By rising from a human death, Christ pushes back the darkness of sin and shows us the light of God's great love. It is in the glory of his resurrection that Jesus comes into his messiahship. Now the followers of Jesus may proclaim him. After Pentecost, when the Spirit filled the apostles and they began their ministries, Peter proclaimed to the crowds that God promised the resurrection of the Messiah from the house of David.

NCD

"In carrying out His earthly mission as the Messiah, Jesus fulfilled Old Testament prophecy and history. He preached the gospel of the kingdom of God and summoned people to interior conversion and faith (cf. Mk 1,15). He persisted in His ministry despite resistance, threats, and apparent failure.

"Out of filial love for His Father (cf. Jn 14,31) and redemptive love for us, He gave Himself up to death (cf. Gal 2,20; 1 Jn 3,16) and passed through death to the glory of the Father (cf. Phil 2,9ff; Eph 1,20)" (No. 90).

VATICAN II

"Jesus Christ was sent into the world as the true Mediator between God and men. . . . The Son of man did not come to be served, but to serve and to give his life as a ransom for many, that is for all. . . . Christ, whom the Father sanctified and sent into the world (cf. Jn. 10:36), said of himself: 'The Spirit of the Lord is upon me, because he anointed me; to bring good news to the poor he sent me, to heal the broken-hearted, to proclaim to the captive release, and sight to the blind' " (Decree on the Church's Missionary Activity, No. 3).

> "God raised this man Jesus to life, and all of us are witnesses to that. . . . For this reason the whole House of Israel can be certain that God has made this Jesus whom you crucified both Lord and Christ" (Acts 2:32,36).

Christ's total, dedicated love of his father results in the redeeming of each of us who will make the same response. God's master plan of creation and salvation is complete. But, we must never think of salvation as a once-in-a-lifetime deal made at baptism. Our salvation in Jesus demands a constant rebirth in faith throughout our lives. Our relationship with God must be a living and growing one; otherwise, like any neglected relationship it will wither and die.

> My dear people,
> let us love one another
> since love comes from God
> and everyone who loves is begotten of God and knows God.
> Anyone who fails to love can never have known God,
> because God is love.
> God's love for us was revealed
> when God sent into the world his only Son
> so that we could have life through him (1 Jn 4:7-9).

DID JESUS HAVE ALLERGIES?

I must confess that I have watched many a teachable moment pass by, not really knowing what to do with it, but one possible success relating to the nature of Christ went as follows:

Amy was suffering from a series of headaches, and allergies were discussed as the

possible cause. After several days of this, while pondering over a bowl of Cheerios, Amy popped the question, "Did Jesus have allergies?" Her expression seemed to show concern for Jesus and the pure curiosity of a child. But she seemed to have a much deeper concern than the state of Jesus' health. She was in fact questioning if Christ was human. Was he subject to her illness? Did he feel her pain?

We spoke for several minutes about Jesus the man, fully human, completely vulnerable to pain and illness. Jesus of Nazareth, a carpenter's son, a laborer, a small-town person. We spoke about what he might have looked like, what he wore, what he might have done as a child. And Jesus seemed to take on a personal reality for Amy. We surmised that he may very well have had allergies.

The church has always taught that Jesus was fully human and fully divine, and like all Christians, children are convinced of Christ's divinity. In general, though, it is more difficult for them to fully accept his humanity. Indeed, many heresies have originated from our inability to fathom the mystery of Jesus' equally human and divine nature. But it cheats the passion and the mission of our Savior to deny him his human thoughts, feelings, heritage and, quite possibly, his allergies.

As parents, we need to be open to the fact that sometimes our own children, in their innocence and unspoiled view of life, can be powerful messengers of Christ's message of love and hope.

LIGHT IN THE DARKNESS

Paul, one of our closest friends, and I met when we were college classmates in the seminary. He was a gifted scholar who graduated summa cum laude. His intellectual achievements were surpassed, however, by his great charisma in dealing with other people, regardless of their own level of knowledge or experience. Paul was always able to attune himself to the people with whom he was dealing. He was both liked and respected throughout the school, and was called upon to serve in numerous capacities of campus and community leadership.

After graduation Paul and I remained close, even though I joined the Navy and Paul continued in the seminary. When my wife and I were married, Paul was best man. He is also the godfather of all three of our children.

When the Navy sent me off to study languages, it happened to be to the same area where Paul had been sent to continue his seminary training. We tried to spend as much time as we could together, and he became a member of the family. We would get together for dinner whenever possible, or he would just drop by to talk and visit with us. At the time, we had only our first son, still a small child, and Paul loved to play with him.

Over a period of time it became obvious to us that Paul seemed to be under more and more of a strain. His talents had been recognized by the school, and he had taken on numerous leadership roles and a full load of theological studies. He laughed it off, but we could see that all these

responsibilities were taking a toll. Eventually, Paul realized the burdens were too great and tried unsuccessfully to cut back. His health began to suffer and we could literally see him weakening. It was particularly obvious to us when after an absence of a week or so, we saw how drawn and pale he looked. We were really frustrated, because there didn't seem to be anything more that we could do except love Paul and continue to be there for him when he needed us. Finally, another friend from college and I, along with our families, planned a surprise weekend in the mountains to get Paul out of the city and "away from it all." But on the very Friday we were to leave, Paul suffered a breakdown. He left for home the next day for extensive medical treatment.

I felt angry. Angry at the school for not seeing what was happening to Paul. Angry at myself for not being able to do more to help. And angry at God for letting it happen.

Ever so slowly, Paul returned to health, surrounded by his loving family at home. I finished my language studies and we went home for a short vacation before going overseas. During the visit, Paul and I talked about what had happened. He said that as he looked back on his blackest days of fatigue and depression, he remembered all the things we had tried to do to help him. He knew intellectually that he was surrounded by people who knew and loved him deeply, people who were trying their best to ease his suffering. But he said that his heart and spirit did not, or could not, accept it. But he said that in all that darkness, there was one ray of light—one

VATICAN II

"This love is not something reserved for important matters, but must be exercised above all in the ordinary circumstances of daily life. Christ's example in dying for us sinners teaches us that we must carry the cross, which the flesh and the world inflict on the shoulders of all who seek after peace and justice. Constituted Lord by his resurrection and given all authority in heaven and on earth, Christ is now at work in the hearts of men by the power of his Spirit; not only does he arouse in them a desire for the world to come but he quickens, purifies, and strengthens the generous aspirations of mankind to make life more humane and conquer the earth for this purpose" (Pastoral Constitution on the Church in the Modern World, No. 38).

person from whom he encountered unquestioning and total love and support. That person was our son.

I was awestruck! First, I had never sensed a profound relationship between Paul and Tommy. There was an obvious and loving bond there such as you might see between an uncle and nephew, but nothing more. I was also surprised that Christ was so alive in Tommy to convey to Paul that he was loved, without fanfare or great outward displays of affection, but rather just for being himself. Christ had accomplished through Tommy what the rest of us had been unable to do. I felt joy and humility that both Paul and Tommy had been touched by the Lord in this experience.

I believe that Tommy was God's messenger to Paul, not because of any special abilities, but because Tommy could show Paul a complete and undemanding childlike love. By doing that, he became a ray of light in the darkness surrounding Paul.

III

THE SPIRIT MOVES

> Since the Spirit is our life, let us be directed by the Spirit (Gal 5:25).

The First Pentecost

A group of men and women huddled in a room. They were afraid, feeling alone and abandoned. They had known a man who said he was God, who predicted his own death and resurrection, then died and rose. These men and women had seen miracles, had listened to teachings and near the end they had accepted a commission to share these teachings with all people. After his death they had walked and talked with Jesus. And yet, in their locked room they were afraid, they felt inadequate. They were frozen into inaction. Then—

> Suddenly they heard what sounded like a powerful wind from heaven, the noise of which filled the entire house in which they were sitting; and something appeared to them that seemed like tongues of fire; these separated and came to rest on the head of each of them. They were filled with the Holy Spirit and began to speak foreign languages as the Spirit gave them the gift of speech (Acts 2:1-4).

Jesus had promised that he would send an advocate (Jn 14:16). Until this advocate came, the apostles were bound by their own human frailty. But after they were "filled with the Spirit" they became alive and purposeful. They preached, cured and baptized. They were renewed and began a new church.

Our Pentecost

The same Spirit which came to the apostles comes to us. Without this Spirit of God we are left to our human means. It is the Spirit who inspires us, guides us, unites us, and teaches us. Without him we are essentially left in a situation of at best humanism and at worst absurd isolation.

The only way for the apostles to leave their fear and isolation was to accept the presence of God in their lives, leave their room and move out in action. Like the apostles, we also have only one course: living in the Spirit through involvement in the community of Christ. And it is we as parents who will initiate, encourage and nurture that involvement for our children. We must constantly pray to, with, and in the Holy Spirit that we will be effective instruments of his activating force, directing our children toward a response to Christ. The purpose of the Spirit is to show us the way to Christ.

Isolation can assume many forms. We can lock ourselves in a protective room of indifference, hate, fear, or self-love. But when we allow God into our lives, his Spirit becomes a strength for us. As parents we have a particular charter to foster the presence of God in us and to act in the belief of that divine presence. Thereby we are models to our children. But who says we are called to action? Who says we must do anything more than believe and remain in our safely locked rooms?

Scripture does:

My children,
our love is not to be just words or mere talk,
but something real and active (1 Jn 3:18).

Do realize, you senseless man, that faith without good deeds is useless (Jas 2:20).

VATICAN II

"The discovery of intimacy with God, the necessity for adoration, the need for intercession—the experience of Christian holiness shows us the fruitfulness of prayer, in which God reveals himself to the spirit and heart of his servants. The Lord gives us this knowledge of himself in the fervor of love. The gifts of the Spirit are many, but they always grant us a taste of that true and intimate knowledge of the Lord" (Apostolic Exhortation on the Renewal of Religious Life, No. 43).

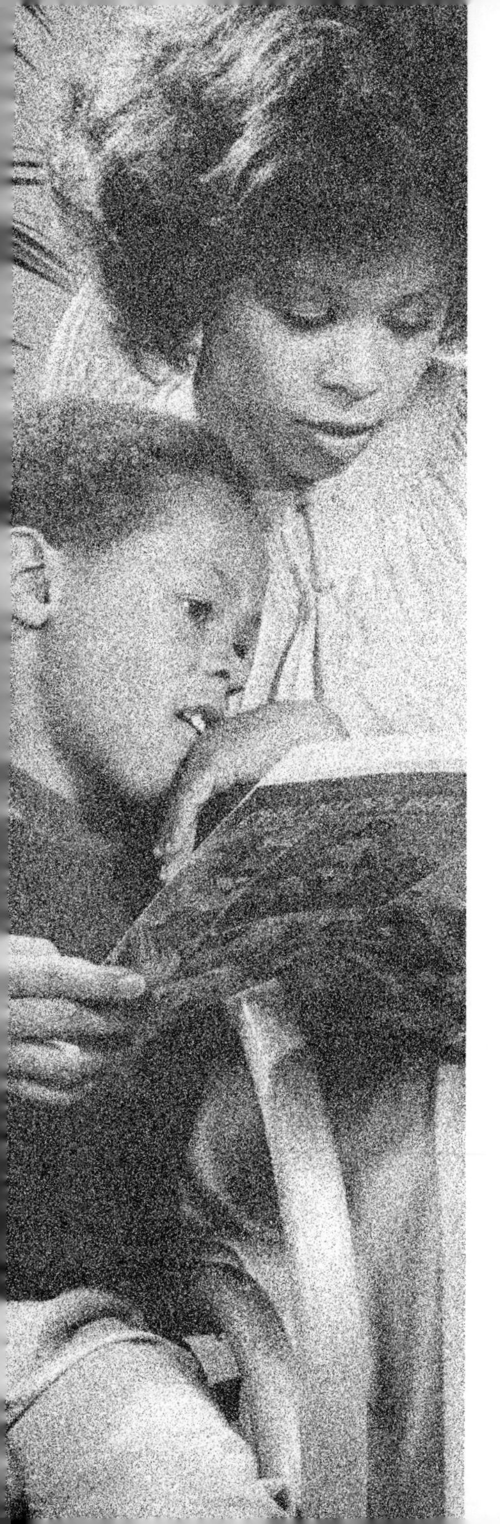

"I know all about you: how you are neither cold nor hot. I wish you were one or the other, but since you are neither, but only lukewarm, I will spit you out of my mouth" (Rev 3:15-16).

And the church does (through the words of the Second Vatican Council):

> No less fervent a zeal on the part of lay people is called for today; present circumstances, in fact, demand from them an apostolate infinitely broader and more intense.
>
> The need for this urgent and many-sided apostolate is shown by the manifest action of the Holy Spirit moving laymen today to a deeper and deeper awareness of their responsibility and urging them on everywhere to the service of Christ and the Church.
>
> The Council, then, makes to all the laity an earnest appeal in the Lord to give a willing, noble and enthusiastic response to the voice of Christ, who at this hour is summoning them more pressingly, and to the urging of the Holy Spirit (Decree on the Apostolate of Lay People, Nos. 1, 33).

But even more persuasive than the imperatives of scripture and the church are the results of how the Spirit works in our life and consequently in our family. The more we open ourselves to the Spirit, the more we participate in his fruits.

> What the Spirit brings is very different: love, joy, peace, patience, kindness, goodness, trustfulness, gentleness and self-control (Gal 5:23).

As we open ourselves to the Spirit in prayer, we find the sacraments, scripture reading, and the teachings of the church become more a part of our lives. The Spirit is unlimited, but we aren't. So we must grow day by day in our ability to receive him, learning how to apply the fruits he provides.

The Continuous Pentecost

The fruits of the Holy Spirit are experienced as individual virtues which each Christian can express in his or her own fashion. Perhaps even more mystical is the manner in which the Spirit moves in the church. The most striking analogy for this effect is the Body of Christ (1 Cor 12), which compares the various parts of the body to individual members of the church. Each has its own function, each depends on other parts of the body for its existence. And it is the Spirit which is the life source of the body—the nervous system, the brain and soul all in one. This analogy stresses the interdependence of Christians on one another and on the sustaining force of the Spirit.

It also portrays the concept of the gifts of the Spirit. These gifts are the special talents which each Christian possesses but which are given specifically to nurture the body of Christ. As members of the body we each have one or more gifts which are required by the body. "The eye cannot say to the hand, 'I do not need you,' nor can the head say to the feet, 'I do not need you' " (1 Cor 12:21). We are freely given our talents, our gifts, or our graces. They are truly supernatural in nature, be they preaching, healing, leading, building, teaching, counseling, consoling, or prophesying.

But we are called to exhibit these gifts in a specific place in a particular time to a unique group of people. And so our gifts are transformed into supportive actions of ushering the 9:00 a.m. Mass, instructing a CCD class, being secretary of the mothers' club, cleaning the church, lectoring, commentating, keeping the church books.

VATICAN II

"The Spirit dwells in the Church and in the hearts of the faithful, as in a temple (cf. 1 Cor. 3:16; 6:19). In them he prays and bears witness to their adoptive sonship (cf. Gal. 4:6; Rom. 8:15-16 and 26). Guiding the Church in the way of all truth (cf. Jn. 16:13), and unifying her in communion and in the works of ministry, he bestows on her varied hierarchic and charismatic gifts, and in this way directs her; and he adorns her with his fruits" (Dogmatic Constitution on the Church, No. 4).

NCD

"While the Spirit animates the whole of creation and permeates the lives of human beings, He is present in a special way in the Church, the community of those who recognize Christ as Lord. Our lives are to be guided by the same Holy Spirit, the third person of the Trinity" [No. 92].

VATICAN II

"As all the members of the human body, though they are many, form one body, so also are the faithful in Christ (cf. 1 Cor. 12:12). Also, in the building up of Christ's body there is engaged a diversity of members and functions. There is only one Spirit who, according to his own richness and the needs of the ministries, gives his different gifts for the welfare of the Church (cf. 1 Cor. 12:1-11). Among these gifts the primacy belongs to the grace of the apostles to whose authority the Spirit himself subjects even those who are endowed with charisms (cf. 1 Cor. 14). Giving the body unity through himself, both by his own power and by the interior union of the members, this same Spirit produces and stimulates love among the faithful. From this it follows that if one member suffers anything, all the members suffer with him, and if one member is honored, all the members together rejoice (cf. 1 Cor. 12:26)" (Dogmatic Constitution on the Church, No. 7).

"Gifts of the Holy Spirit" sounds majestic, certainly more so than directing traffic after a parish youth basketball game, but we each have a special way or ways in which we support the body. This is not to suggest that the gifts of some members are mundane and others are of a higher order. They are each required by the body. "If one part is hurt, all parts are hurt with it. If any part is given special honor, all parts enjoy it" (1 Cor 12:26).

Also, this does not suggest that we are limited to using our gifts only in a parish environment. The nurse who takes an extra minute to care for a patient is a physical and a spiritual healer—so too is the priest who anoints the patient. The worker who lets Christian views be known in a secular environment is a prophet. The parent discussing a major decision with a child is a counselor. The conglomerate of these gifts, the aggregate of the graces, for better or worse, is the body of Christ. It is only as good or as failing as we are at accepting the gifts of the Spirit and living the gifts for one another.

No study of doctrine, no theology and no catechism will prepare us to help our children to come into a relationship with God. It is the Spirit of God that moves us in these matters. What we need in order to work with our children is:

Love: Our effectiveness in nurturing our children will to a large extent be measured by their perception of our love for them.

Joy: If it is not fun, neither we nor the kids will be able to sustain it.

Peace: We must be comfortable with talking about God, so first we must be comfortable with God.

Patience: And lots of it.

Kindness: Christ did not teach in a harsh or stern manner. He practiced what he preached, and he preached kindness.

Goodness: Our lives are teaching examples. In the final analysis our children learn more from what we do than from what we say.

Trustfulness: Our children must sense a community in their family. They must feel secure to be receptive to our message.

Gentleness: Here again the Lord is our example.

Self-Control: It's not easy to perform our functions as the primary educators of our children. It means a sacrifice of time and effort. It takes no small amount of persistence.

The Spirit has been described in this chapter as an active force who draws us out of self-filled loneliness, brings us closer to Christ and moves us to act in response to Christ's love. In our families, we are encouraged to open ourselves to the power of the Spirit.

A CHILD'S LETTERS

Often I have forgotten that children are people, with a full set of feelings and emotions. This was made very real to me when I found the following letters written by my daughter.

Letter 1. "You know what God? I think nobody cares about me, ya know what I mean God? Like left out ya know God. You're a pretty good guy. Please kind of melt me into the family again; it would be very nice, because I feel very

lonely ya know. God will you please help me? I mean I'm not saying that I don't like how you made life on earth, but I just don't like the way you made mine. Oh God please help me. I mean I still love you and all the things you made on this wonderful earth. I just don't like how you made me. I think you made a mistake by putting me on this earth or planet. The whole world is ruined just because you put me on the earth."

Letter 2. "God, I love you very much. And I love my mom and dad very much too, and I hate my big brother. He picks on me too much. God, when I look out the window and see all the lights on it sort of brightens your heart. And when they're all turned out it sort of breaks your heart. And that's the way I feel when I get left out. You know, you feel kind of died out. You know what I mean, you feel sort of died out?"

At first I was embarrassed and felt guilty that my own daughter was feeling such abandonment. Yet, I was encouraged by her ability to articulate those feelings. I prayed. I prayed that my own feelings of guilt would cease so that I could concentrate on her need for love. I prayed for wisdom and peace so that I could openly accept her when she felt ready to rejoin the family.

Later in the day, we discussed her loneliness. Nothing I said made the situation better, but as I stopped talking and listened to her discuss her feelings I could see the load lifting from her. The Spirit began to work as she saw that she and her feelings were readily accepted. Eventually she literally talked herself back into the family. We ended with a prayer.

NCD

"Children begin to be segregated from their parents in the first years of life, and this isolation continues through preschool. . . .

"As adults give less time to parenting, young people respond by creating a youth subculture, whose values and attitudes are dictated largely by television and peers instead of parents and teachers.

"In view of the intrinsic importance of parents and family in transmitting cultural and religious attitudes and values, this isolation of infants, children and youth poses major problems for catechesis. . . . Of special importance is family catechesis, where young people can spend 'quality time' with parents or guardians" (No. 197).

GRACE

Bless us, O Lord, and these thy gifts which—Ring—we are about—Russ will you get that?—to receive from thy—It's for Amy—bounty, through Christ our Lord—Tell her to call back—Amen.

"How was school, Amy?"

"Junk!"

"How did the test go?"

"Pass the peas."

"Say please."

"Peas please."

"Bad news. Mrs. Hall always asks trick questions; I got a 78."

"Did you study?"

"Russ, get your stupid foot off my chair."

"It's the dog, dummy!"

"Where's my knife?"

"I don't have a fork."

"Amy must have set the table."

At this point I realized what a disaster the meal was becoming. I opened myself to the Spirit, asked for patience and wisdom, and. . . . "Wait! I can't handle this; we're all just blurting out. Let's take a minute, be very quiet and think of something to be thankful for."

Mom started: "I'm thankful for the letter I received today; it really picked me up."

"I'm thankful for the 78; without studying it could have been a lot worse."

"I'm thankful for the new team uniforms."

"I'm thankful for peaceful moments like this."

IV

THE FAMILY IN PRAYER

"I tell you solemnly once again, if two of you on earth agree to ask for anything at all, it will be granted to you by my Father in heaven. For where two or three meet in my name, I shall be there with them" (Mt 18:19-20).

Before we talk about prayer in the family, we would like to look briefly at what prayer is, or should be. Many of us learned from the Baltimore Catechism that "prayer is the lifting of our minds and hearts to God." While there is truth in that definition, it is incomplete. First, in this definition, God seems remote. Secondly, prayer seems a one-way street: We lift our minds and hearts to God—then what?

Vatican II addressed these very issues in its Decree on the Renewal of Religious Life. The Council Fathers referred to prayer as "the discovery of *intimacy* with God . . . in which *God reveals himself* to the spirit and heart of his servants. The Lord gives us this knowledge of himself in the *fervor of love*" (emphasis added, Apostolic Exhortation on the Renewal of Religious Life, No. 43). Even more recently the American bishops described prayer as "a deepening awareness of our covenanted relationship with God, coupled with the effort to live in total harmony with His will" (*NCD*, No. 140). In trying to piece together the key points of all these views and our own experiences, we came up with this definition: *Prayer is a loving conversation with God that matures with practice and inspires us to Christian action.*

NCD

"Because Christ's revelation is inexhaustible, we can always know more about it and understand it better (cf. Eph 3,18ff). We grow in such knowledge and understanding when we respond to God manifesting Himself through creation, the events of daily life, the triumphs and tragedies of history. God speaks to us in a special manner in His word—sacred scripture—and through prayer, communicating His love and beauty to us through the Holy Spirit" (No. 55).

Just like any conversation, prayer can be experienced in a variety of ways and for any number of reasons. Do you remember this question from the Baltimore Catechism?

Q. Why do we pray?

A. We pray:
First, to adore God, expressing to Him our love and loyalty.
Second, to thank Him for His favors.
Third, to obtain from Him the pardon of our sins and the remission of their punishment.
Fourth, to ask for graces and blessings for ourselves and others.

Even though many things have changed since those days, the church still teaches that "there are four general purposes of prayer: adoration, thanksgiving, petition, and contrition. As a life of prayer matures it becomes more simple, and adoration, thanksgiving, and contrition tend to predominate" (*NCD*, No. 140).

Let's take a closer look at these basic functions of prayer.

Adoration

Praise Yahweh, all nations,
extol him, all you peoples!
For his love is strong,
his faithfulness eternal (Ps 117).

In the face of God's goodness and love, what else can we do but offer praise? Praise is a spontaneous uplifting of our minds and emotions, a natural response to the glory of God. It can be public or private. We don't have to practice praise to be good at it. Rather, like most forms of communication, we simply have to remove our preconceptions and inhibitions. Perhaps the greatest gift we can give our children is the exam-

SCRIPTURE

"I tell you therefore: everything you ask and pray for, believe that you have it already, and it will be yours" (Mk 11:24).

VATICAN II

"The Christian is indeed called to pray with others, but he must also enter into his bedroom to pray to his Father in secret; furthermore, according to the teaching of the apostle, he must pray without ceasing" (The Constitution on the Sacred Liturgy, No. 12).

SCRIPTURE

"Glory for ever to Yahweh!
May Yahweh find joy in what he creates,
at whose glance the earth trembles,
at whose touch the mountains smoke!
"I mean to sing to Yahweh all my life,
I mean to play for my God as long as I live" (Ps 104:31-33).

"Be happy at all times; pray constantly; and for all things give thanks to God, because this is what God expects you to do in Christ Jesus" (1 Thes 5:16-18).

ple of spontaneous praise. Scripture gives excellent advice on offering praise. The Psalms are full of exhortations for joyful, musical, enthusiastic singing, and singing is a natural hit with children and an effective spiritual tool for the Christian parent.

Praise the Lord; your son will praise with you,
Praise the Lord; your daughter will sing too.
Praise the Lord; joy will live with you,
Praise the Lord; now and forever.

Thanksgiving

Walk through his porticos giving thanks,
enter his courts praising him,
give thanks to him, bless his name (Ps 100).

The Lord blesses us constantly. When we stop to consider this and literally count our blessings, we realize that a continuous attitude of thanks is not at all inappropriate. But given our day-to-day schedules, we seem to find it necessary to distill our thanksgiving into capsules of thought or prayer which we offer to God. This is not to say that thanksgiving cannot be impromptu. Indeed, families can and should give thanks in whatever ways seem comfortable.

Petition

"Ask, and it will be given to you; search, and you will find; knock, and the door will be opened to you" (Mt 7:7).

Petitioning God is perhaps our most common prayer. If we are to become accomplished petitioners there are a couple of basic principles we need to know:

1. God wants us to ask for whatever we need, and he answers our prayers.

2. The answer to our prayers may not be exactly what we expected.

THE BASEBALL

I had been separated from my family on a military assignment for an extended period of time and when I returned my son and I went to a baseball game. A friend had recently emphasized the importance of praying for the little things in life, something which I had never done. But his encouragement led me to pray for a baseball for my son. Now, that may seem a pretty trivial thing to pray for; but when you have been away from your family for a long time, these little things take on added significance. I could picture myself protectively catching the ball and then handing it to my son.

By the bottom of the ninth inning I was beginning to worry, but using my friend's advice I put aside any doubt and claimed the answer to my prayer. Deep down, I realized that the baseball was really a symbol for the love I wanted to give to my son, the love I had not been able to show him tangibly for so long. Suddenly, a foul tip was heading our way. It was a high pop and I would have little trouble handling it. But then I saw that it was falling short. "Further," I yelled, as if to incite the Holy Spirit. My heart sank when the ball hit three rows in front of us and then bounced over our heads! But as I turned to see where it was landing I saw that Russell had run back and caught the ball!

How beautifully my prayer was answered. Russell had the ball; together we had a marvelous experience, and I had a lesson in prayer:

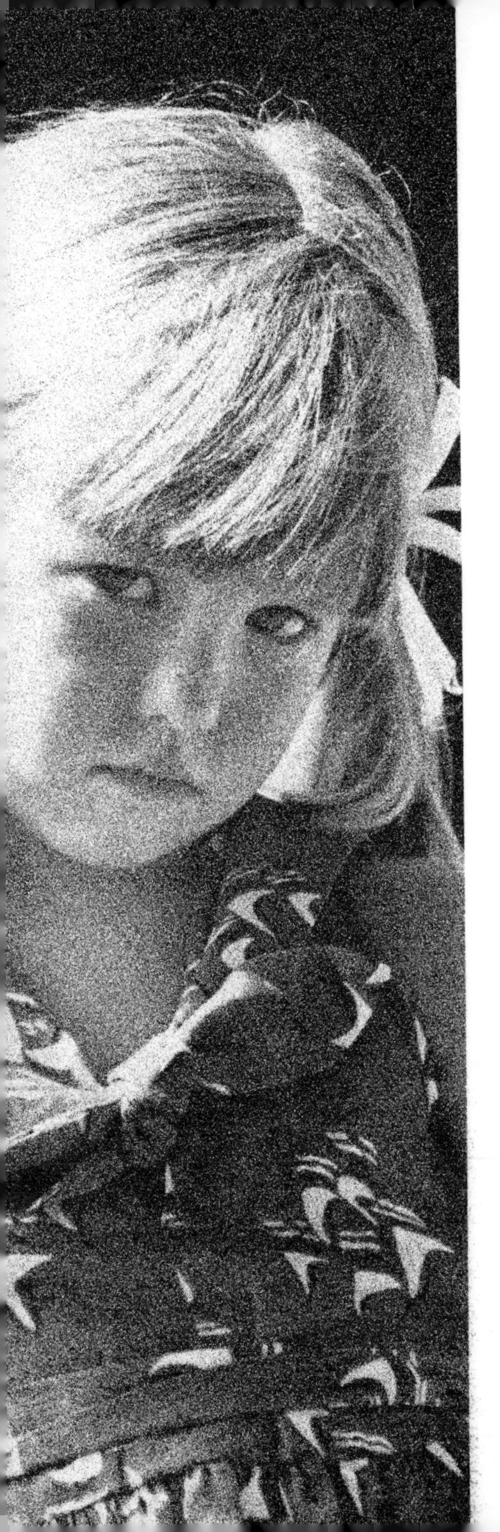

—**God really does answer specific prayers of petition, even for the little things.**
—**He may not answer in the way I expect him to.**
—**He doesn't need me to convey his answers.**

Contrition

As humans we fail continuously. In countless ways, small and large, we knowingly fail to respond to God's call to love. When children begin to accept responsibility for these failings, they can easily feel very defeated. But through contrition and reconciliation, this defeat can turn into a joyful, healing experience. This phenomenon works well on a purely human level:

> "If your brother does something wrong, reprove him and, if he is sorry, forgive him. And if he wrongs you seven times a day, and seven times comes back to you and says, 'I am sorry,' you must forgive him" (Lk 17:3-4).

God constantly offers us forgiveness, and there is never any doubt of our being forgiven when we are truly sorry. The life of Christ offers many examples of God's forgiving nature. Indeed, the very act of sending his son as our salvation is an act of God's great forgiveness:

> "Yes, God loved the world so much
> that he gave his only Son,
> so that everyone who believes in him may not be
> lost
> but may have eternal life.
> For God sent his Son into the world
> not to condemn the world,
> but so that through him the world might be
> saved" (Jn 3:16-17).

Where do children learn to forgive and to ask for forgiveness? Parents, of course, are the primary representatives of God's forgiveness. This does not mean that children do not need to be reprimanded and at times punished! It does mean that they should always be forgiven. Reconciliation is as important as the punishment, if not more so. Children should be offered forgiveness shortly after punishment, often a difficult task for an upset parent. A prayer which joins parent and child in seeking reconciliation can be effective as long as the child feels open to it.

SCRIPTURE

"When you stand in prayer, forgive whatever you have against anybody, so that your Father in heaven may forgive your failings too" (Mk 11:25).

NCD

"Catechesis for prayer begins very early in childhood by hearing others pray" (No. 145).

Some Principles of Family Prayer

Now we will look at some principles of prayer in the family. This is by no means an exhaustive list; rather, it contains things that we have experienced in our families' prayer lives, and we offer them for your consideration.

1. Parents are the key.

How many parents do you know who are content to sit back and let their children come to them with religious ideas that they may have heard in school or CCD class? A good friend of ours once told us how he got involved with his kids when they were preparing to receive a sacrament. "Oh sure," he said, "I get involved. The school sends home these real good pamphlets on confession and communion, and I make sure the kids read them. It's really great." This man is a well-educated executive. In any other aspect of his children's upbringing, he would not exhibit such a cavalier attitude. But he is like many well-intentioned parents, who fail to realize their duty in the spiritual formation of their children, or think themselves too ignorant to do the job. We need to remember that Christ came to each of us. His apostles were fishermen, and his message was simple: Turn away from hatred and fear, and turn back to the love of God.

We also need to examine what our own feelings and experiences have taught us about prayer and spirituality. Every individual has been formed by a different set of experiences.

We all come to our families from different prayer backgrounds and different types of prayer experience. As couples and as parents, we have to re-examine our own prayer lives in order to create a meaningful prayer environment for each of us within our families. Finally, we must constantly study and grow in our own spirituality as adults and as individuals. The more we grow in faith and loving dialogue with God, the more we can contribute to the overall growth of the family.

SCRIPTURE

"If you have faith, everything you ask for in prayer you will receive" (Mt 21:22).

NCD

"Whether communal or individual, all strivings in prayer are efforts to associate ourselves as consciously and consistently as possible with the constant activity of the Spirit dwelling within us" (No. 140).

"Biblical prayer, involving reading scripture and meditating on it, is highly attractive to many today. Some learn favorite psalms and canticles by heart and base private prayer on them" (No. 143).

2. Call God Father.

Prayer should be expressed in intimate and loving terms. This means encouraging each family member to experience Jesus as a person, a brother. It means conversing with God in joy and humor. Obviously by humor we don't mean disrespect, but a good healthy ability to laugh at oneself and the foibles of everyday life. Not only is this healthy from a psychological standpoint, it also impresses children with the fact that God is interested in all of their lives, including the funny parts. Christ himself tells us to be on intimate terms with God. Not only does he tell us to call God "Our Father," he tells us to call him "*Abba*," which is an Aramaic term most accurately translated as "Dad."

3. Every family is unique.

Family prayer should be planned to use particular family interests and strengths, taking into account the ages of the members. Obviously it is not advisable for a family with preschoolers to kneel down after supper and pray 15 decades of the rosary. However, walking on the beach and sharing the problems of the day with the Lord and one another might be just right for a family with grade- or high-schoolers. Find your own best vehicles for prayer. Music can be used, as can drama and reading. Use what is right for you. Prayer should be a conscious effort, but not a self-conscious one. Just because another family you know is using a certain type of prayer service with great success does not mean that your family will be able to.

CHILDREN AND PRAYER

Each of our children has developed his or her own prayer personality. We have Jennifer the Hugger, Stephen the Tickler, and Thomas the Thinker.

Not long ago, Grandma and Grandpa sent 3-year-old Jennifer a delightful book which describes and illustrates a variety of hugs. It includes octopus hugs, blanket hugs, people hugs, and gives a lot of interesting "facts" and hints about hugs. The book really struck a chord in Jenny, and she began trying out all these hugs on us. When I leave the house for work I have to be careful not to be tackled by a "knee hug" enthusiastically applied by the Hugger. All this hugging has carried over into our prayer life. Jenny is usually the first person to reach out to hold hands during a family prayer. Her desire for the cuddling and intimacy she has known since birth is developing into an awareness that people need to touch one another at important times to ex-

press unity and love. She is learning that prayer is such a time.

Stephen, 8, is the Tickler. He is by nature a quiet person, shy and easily embarrassed. So it took us by surprise when he emerged as the instigator of our "tickle parties." Naturally, it is a great way for a reserved person to get the same physical display of attention and affection that he thinks he is too big to ask for directly. We have made use of this fact in a variety of ways with Stephen, including prayer. The tickling serves to "prime the pump" for prayer: Stephen lets his guard down, feels the warmth and love he wants, and loses his fear. In this atmosphere, he is then disposed for a loving talk with God.

The Thinker is 10. Tom is very outgoing and enjoys trying new things. Given this fact, he has also taken his share of lumps. As he grows in experience, Tom is developing a more sophisticated sense of community and prayer. He verbalizes easily, and is great with spontaneous prayer: If Jenny is the one who initiates the hand-holding, and Stephen initiates the openness, Tom usually initiates the prayer itself. On the other hand, he also sometimes just wants an arm around his shoulders, or to sit quietly in moments of reflective prayer. He is developing into a more complex person, and this is reflected in his approach to prayer.

What is gratifying is the sight of each of the children growing in prayer according to their emotional growth. We also feel that their ease with physical as well as spiritual expressions of prayer indicates an awareness of God's intimate and constant presence within each of us and among us as family.

---

4. Use meal times for prayer.

Meals offer a unique opportunity for family prayer. We can pray before and after, and the meal itself can be a form of the eucharistic meal. Sharing what went into the preparation of the meal, how everybody did something to make it happen, the love that can be generated during a meal—all make it a natural place for prayer. At no time in the day will more family members be in the same spot. The meal itself is a physical sign of God's benevolence and providence.

We often use the grace before meals period for each family member to express gratitude for the specific gifts of the day. While the parents sometimes take the lead in order to set the mood and give examples, many times the children are bubbling over with things to share.

5. Prayer develops over time.

Family prayer—like any other form of prayer—will grow as the members grow in age, experience, and the art of praying. We parents need to be aware of this evolution and let it happen. This means we must be open to new or different forms of prayer that may develop within the home. There is nothing wrong with trial and error. In fact, the simple act of faith and love which is demonstrated by trying something new is a prayer itself.

6. Use scripture.

Scripture offers an endless variety of applications for prayer depending on the level of development and the age of the members of the family. Retelling Christ's parables in contemporary terms is fun, educational and prayerful for the storyteller and the audience. Certain passages can be read by the family, with each member taking a certain role. Or you can devise a mini-

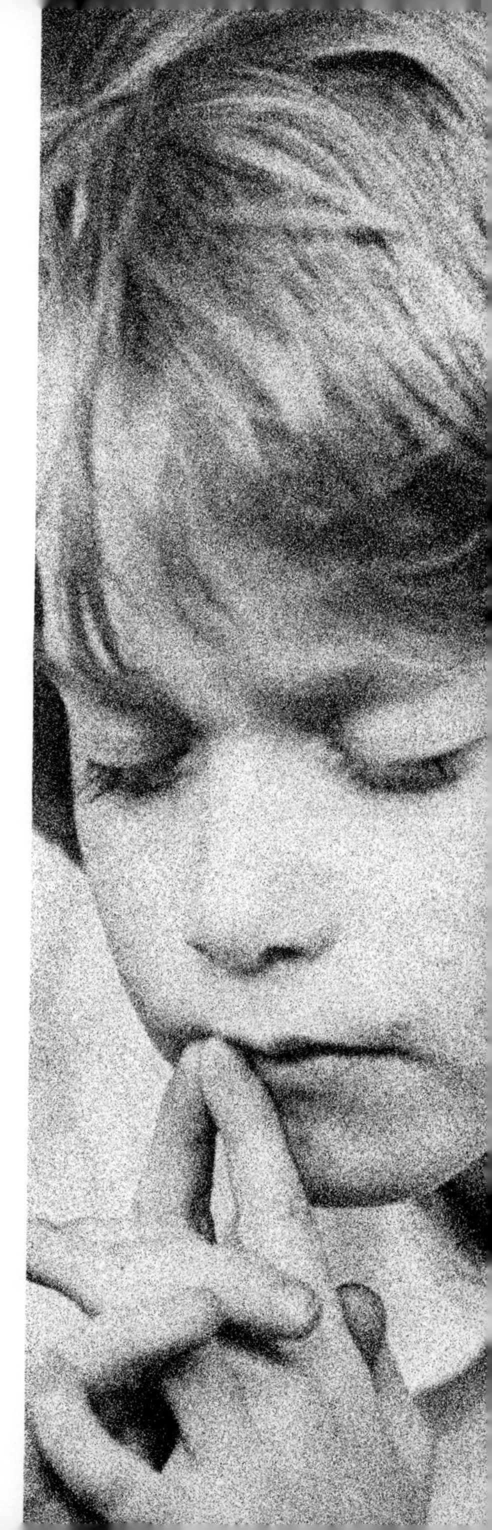

SCRIPTURE

"Pray all the time, asking for what you need, praying in the Spirit on every possible occasion. Never get tired of staying awake to pray for all the saints" (Eph 6:18).

"Everything will soon come to an end, so, to pray better, keep a calm and sober mind" (1 Pt 4:7).

scripture service in which the family gathers around a lit candle and listens to a psalm of thanksgiving and a short reading from the gospels. This can then be followed by a short discussion on the passages that were read and possible applications to family life. Younger children seem to prefer a fairly constant format: This allows them to grow comfortable with the ritual. The content, however, can vary greatly. But none of these suggestions is workable unless parents are willing to continue their own study of scripture and then tailor what they encounter within the word to their own family situation. Obviously, the older the children get, the more they can get involved in this process. You may find that you have your own bible study class right in your own home!

7. Use everyday events.

Everyday things seem to lend themselves to more informal, spontaneous prayer, while more formal feasts like anniversaries, birthdays, and graduations can lead to more formal prayer. The key point is to seize any and every aspect of our lives as an opportunity to converse with God.

8. Touch.

Touching can be very important. In our families we find that holding hands adds a depth of feeling to certain prayer events. A great source of joy can be found in a family hug. Everybody just gathers around and hangs on! It's a fantastic way to come together for a quick prayer before leaving the house in the morning, or for ending the day. The children also enjoy periodic tickle parties in which we all take part. And while the tickle party itself may not be a prayer, the warmth and joy that is felt when it is over can be easily transformed into a cozy prayer of thanksgiving and praise.

9. Listen to the Lord.

Silence is a key ingredient in family prayer. Since prayer is a conversation, you can think of silence as a chance for God to talk with us. And when we listen to God in prayer, it's important to listen for *his* response, not the wishful thoughts which we may have. Our earlier story about the baseball is a good example. God's answer to prayer may not always be the answer we want, or it may be in terms we do not expect.

NCD

"In seeking intimacy with God, silence is necessary; for prayer is a conversation, in which one must listen as well as speak" (No. 143).

The Goal of Family Prayer

Imagine any two people in love. What marks them as lovers? What announces to all who see them that they share something deep and special? It is their constant desire to be together. They are together every available moment, and when they can't be together they write love letters and poems, and talk on the phone for hours. Now think of God as our great love. He is constantly reaching out to hold us. All we need to do is reach back. When we think God is not there for us, that is when we have been blinded by sin or human weakness. As families, our conversations with God reflect our ever-growing awareness of God's saving presence in our lives. That awareness, and the actions that result from that awareness, are the goals of family prayer.

THE FEVER

Our daughter had been afflicted with a high fever for several hours. Being experienced parents, we had tried all the standard remedies without success; baby aspirin and cool baths failed to bring the fever down. Finally we decided to make the 30-minute trip to the nearest medical facility, leaving the two boys at home. As we were leaving the house, all of us joined around Jenny and offered a brief, hurried prayer for her health. Before we had driven a mile, I reached over and felt Jenny, and she seemed cooler. Diann agreed, so we turned around and headed home to check Jenny's temperature once more. To our amazement, it had dropped significantly and she was resting much easier. Within an hour, her temperature was back to normal.

THE SPANKING

It was a very bad day. My wife had stayed up very late the night before finishing a paper for nursing school. It was very busy at the office and the boss had rejected a major project saying it needed "more work." I had a second cup of coffee. My daughter called because her bike had a flat tire, so I had to leave work, pick up the kids at school and take them home. I wondered what the boss thought about that.

After dropping the kids off at home, I told them to be quiet, to let Mom sleep, and to rake the yard—a Saturday chore which was three days overdue. Russ called while I was having my fifth cup of coffee to ask if he could make hamburgers for dinner. Finally, the workday was over and I dragged myself home. Turning into the drive, I saw that the yard wasn't raked. Walking up to the front door I heard screaming and loud laughing. How could Mom possibly be getting any sleep? Opening the door, I saw the kids chasing each other through the house, throwing hamburger. The pressure of the day, most of which was self-inflicted, overcame me.

"Where's the ruler?"—no ruler—"Where's the wooden spoon?" Kids being spanked. Mom enters, groggy from sleep, shocked by the scene. Argument about the spanking. Family wrenched apart.

Later that evening the kids and I were able to discuss the spanking. I told them that they deserved the punishment for their actions. They said they were sorry and we were reconciled. I told them that I thought I spanked them too hard and that I was sorry for that. They agreed, especially about the "too hard" part. But their mother was still very upset. She had never seen me that angry, and avoided talking about it all evening. She went to bed alone.

At 2:00 a.m. I was still awake. I couldn't figure it out. I was reading the bible daily, going to Mass, praying. Why should I have been so overwhelmed by such little things? In the peace of the night, in the quiet of my solitude, I prayed:

Father, I am tired.
I am looking for your will.
The family is torn apart;
I seem to be a part of the problem.
I'm sorry.
Send your Spirit; heal me.
Give me strength.

I breathed deeply and became calm. I sat waiting, quietly and receptively thinking. Gradually in retrospect the day became clear. I saw how the pressure had increased; how my ego was involved in it all. I saw the humiliation, the hurt pride, the frustration, the anxiety. I saw that even my caffeine consumption was adding to the problem! Then I slept.

The next day my daughter admitted to having let the air out of her tire so I would have to drive them home. We laughed about it. She was forgiven, and so was I. Although my wife's fear lasted, gradually we were able to discuss the spanking openly and heal the family totally.

V

GOD'S FAMILY: THE CHURCH

What exactly is the church? Some people describe it as a society built around its priests and bishops, an institutional structure. Others describe it as the Mystical Body of Christ. Still others say that the church is a sacrament, a visible sign of Christ in the world. Some emphasize its communal nature, the people of God. Each of these is correct, but not complete. The noted Belgian churchman, Cardinal Suenens, writes:

> A reason for our present tensions is that certain people wish to choose one of these models in such a way that it excludes or dominates the others (*A New Pentecost,* p. 15).

In reality, the church is all of these things, and much more.

Pope Paul VI opened the second session of Vatican II in September 1963 by calling the church "a mystery . . . both divine and human." It is divine because of its divine origin and divine mission. It is human because it is made up of people joined by their shared faith in Christ—the people of God's new covenant.

Social scientists tell us that on a purely human level, we join together to meet our biological, emotional, and psychological needs. Our human communities are based on those things we hold in common: language, law, culture, and history. How much more profound and powerful is that spiritual glue which binds us: the shared faith in a God who loves us so much that he sent his own son to call us back to him! As believers in Christ we live together under the same law:

> "You did not choose me,
> no, I chose you;

NCD

" 'Community' involves a sharing of beliefs, experiences, ideals, and values. Christian community leads one to put aside selfish goals and private interest for the sake of a common good. It is based on the willingness of all community members, as good stewards, to accept responsibility, individually and corporately, for the way each lives, uses his or her time, talent, and treasure, and responds to the needs and rights of others" (No. 70).

> and I commissioned you
> to go out and to bear fruit,
> fruit that will last;
> and then the Father will give you
> anything you ask him in my name.
> What I command you
> is to love one another" (Jn 15:16-17).

In living out this command, we Christians are called to be a community of love, a community of people who acknowledge the loving act of Jesus and answer the divine call to continue his work in our hearts and in our world. By this natural sharing in Christ, we can say with St. Paul:

> The blessing-cup that we bless is a communion with the blood of Christ, and the bread that we break is a communion with the body of Christ. The fact that there is only one loaf means that, though there are many of us, we form a single body because we all have a share in this one loaf (1 Cor 10:16-17).

This one body, therefore, becomes "a chosen race, a royal priesthood, a consecrated nation, a people set apart to sing the praises of God who called you out of the darkness into his wonderful light" (1 Pt 2:9).

The Spirit Within: Tradition and Life

The Holy Spirit is the soul of the church. It is through the Spirit that the people of God grow in love and understanding of God's call. Just before his ascension, Jesus told his apostles not to leave Jerusalem:

> Wait there for what the Father had promised. . . . "You will receive power when the Holy Spirit comes on you and then you will be my witnesses not only in Jerusalem but throughout Judaea and Samaria, and indeed to the ends of the earth" (Acts 1:4, 8).

NCD

"Under the impulse of the Spirit, the Church from its very beginning has been a community of believers. 'Those who believed shared all things in common' (Acts 2,44)" (No. 70).

He also told them,

> "When the Spirit of truth comes
> he will lead you to the complete truth" (Jn 16:13).

Because of Christ's promise to send the Spirit, and the Spirit's continuing presence within us as individuals and as a faith-community, we are able to carry out Christ's command to be his witnesses "to the ends of the earth." The living history of our response to the Spirit is known as sacred tradition. In Chapter I we alluded to the fact that as Catholics we believe that God reveals himself through scripture and tradition. This is based on our faith in the Holy Spirit's active and constant participation in the life of the church.

Our tradition consists of beautiful facets such as the richness of our ritual and the continuity of our history. Our tradition is rooted in the saving act of Christ living and growing through the power of the Spirit. We remain confident in our growth, because as Christ said, the Spirit will guide us to all truth.

Vatican II is a magnificent example of the Spirit—and tradition—at work. The Council took up broad issues such as war and peace, economics, the family—the whole gamut of contemporary social and political concerns—and integrated them into the very fabric of our self-expression as the modern people of God. The Council translated the unchanging word of God into contemporary terms.

> It is the Holy Spirit, then, who works within the shepherds of the Church so that their decisions truly conform to the Gospel, to the life of the Church, and to coming of the Kingdom: and it is he who, at the same time, obliges them to receive and to obey the manifestations of the Spirit which are always present within the whole People of God (*A New Pentecost*, p. 25).

VATICAN II

"The Tradition that comes from the apostles makes progress in the Church, with the help of the Holy Spirit. There is a growth in insight into the realities and words that are being passed on. This comes about in various ways. It comes through the contemplation and study of believers who ponder these things in their hearts (cf. Lk. 2:19 and 51). It comes from the intimate sense of spiritual realities which they experience. And it comes from the preaching of those who have received, along with their right of succession in the episcopate, the sure charism of truth" (Dogmatic Constitution on Divine Revelation, No. 8).

The Individual Within God's Family

Sometimes when we think of the church, it seems easy to think of it as something apart from us. But the church is us. Each and every one of us is responsible for its growth and the success of its mission "to bring about God's kingdom." To continue Paul's analogy of the people of God as the body of Christ:

> The whole body is fitted and joined together, every joint adding its own strength, for each separate part to work according to its function. So the body grows until it has built itself up, in love (Eph 4:16).

As individual Christians, we are called to bear constant witness to Christ in our daily lives: where we live, where we work, and where we play. This is our vocation as Christians. The church, therefore, is not a fortress in which the good are kept sheltered and protected from the bad. Just the opposite. We are called to tear down the walls of fear and isolation. We are called to use our own unique God-given strengths and talents to bring all people to God through Christ.

VATICAN II

"Each individual layman must be a witness before the world to the resurrection and life of the Lord Jesus, and a sign of the living God. All together, and each one to the best of his ability, must nourish the world with spiritual fruits (cf. Gal. 5:22). They must diffuse in the world the spirit which animates those poor, meek and peacemakers whom the Lord in the Gospel proclaimed blessed. In a word: 'what the soul is in the body, let Christians be in the world' " (Dogmatic Constitution on the Church, No. 38).

CHANGE AND FAITH

Bob grew up in a devout Catholic home in the Midwest. His family was heavily involved in the construction trades: the kind of people who thrived on hard work, hard play, and strict adherence to church obligations. Bob went to Catholic grade school, learned his prayers, and spent a lot of time as an altar boy. He enjoyed working in the church, and even thought he'd like to be a priest someday. He found the church to be a warm, comfortable place where everything was clear-cut and all questions had answers.

As he grew older and moved into Catholic high school in the mid-1960s, Bob found that his church was even more comfortable than before because now his outside influences were not so comfortable. There was a lot of peer pressure to get involved in things he knew were wrong. Pressure to succeed academically and socially steadily increased. He found his church to be a safe harbor in which he could be sheltered from the storms raging in the open sea of the real world.

But then those storms hit home. A girlfriend's mother killed herself. Bob, a close friend of the entire family, tried hard to comfort his friend and her family. In the process, he discovered that since the woman committed suicide, the church would not allow her to be buried in a Catholic cemetery or have a Catholic funeral. Bob even talked with the pastor about the situation, explaining how the family needed comfort and understanding. But the pastor's decision remained unchanged.

This was not the church that Bob had grown to accept. That church protected its members from pain; now this church *inflicted* pain! After this, Bob became more aware of things that were starting to bother him about the church. Vatican II had turned the altar around and removed many of the liturgical trappings. The beautiful Latin was gone, as was Gregorian chant. Guitars, good instruments for the Beatles, were now plunking away during Mass and the songs seemed more like folk music than hymns of profound spiritual worship. Sisters were wearing regular clothes, and priests were leading civil rights marches. "The world" was invading his church! Not only

were pressures from the world causing Bob to do a lot of soul-searching, but his own church was adding to the problem.

Now going to a Catholic college, Bob slowly began to adjust to the changes, but he felt he had lost his innocence. Never again would he be able to put priests and nuns on a pedestal; never again would he feel obligated to go to church (after all, the "new theology" said God is in each of us, so why bother with Sunday as long as I'm OK with God). Never again would he be able to accept the judgments of a church that seemed to have lost the ability to make judgments in the first place.

Bob got married (in the church), and moved away after college. Ever critical of the church he had once served so faithfully, Bob slowly drifted away. Sunday Mass became a haphazard thing at best. Confession receded into the mists so far that he soon couldn't even remember the words of the Act of Contrition. When he and his wife did make it to church, he found the priests ill-prepared and inflexible. When the kids came, they were even better reasons for staying away. After all, nobody wants to listen to a screaming baby at church—better stay home.

These were also empty years during which the marriage became shaky. The kids were burdens. Was this all there was to life? This void?

As the kids grew, Bob realized that something had to change or his family would soon disintegrate. He loved his wife and children, but that didn't seem to be enough. God, what could he do now?

God heard Bob's prayer. Gradually, Bob and his wife realized they had to teach their children more about God. Even though they had fallen

away from an active life in the church, they still loved God and felt themselves to be Catholic. So, more for the children's sake than his own, Bob returned to a halfhearted participation in the local parish. Then he began to notice subtle changes in their homelife. Communication between him and his wife improved, and the children seemed to give him greater joy. As their family life began to improve, Bob became more and more active in the church. He began to realize that his voice and his heart were as important to the church as his soul, and that he had a responsibility for the human expression of Christ in the world.

Bob and his family opened themselves to the Spirit and have since blossomed into active, caring Catholic Christians. Of course problems still show up, but now they are more manageable because of their deep faith in the action of God in their lives, and in the lives of their faith-family, the church.

Mission and Ministry

"In the Church there is diversity of ministry but unity of mission" (Decree on the Apostolate of Lay People, No. 2). That means each of us has a job to do, regardless of sex, age, education or profession. Any group of people joined as a community requires that certain functions be performed for the sake of the community at large. We have public servants who administer our societal rules and programs. We have policemen, fire fighters, accountants, construction workers, military personnel, factory workers, presidents, bakers, bankers, farmers, ranchers, artists, mayors, singers, actors, governors, bus drivers,

NCD

"The Church—that community of loving believers in the risen Lord—is called to be a sign of God's kingdom already in our midst. . . .

"To be a sign of the kingdom already here, the Church on every level—most immediately on the parish level—must be committed to justice, love, and peace, to grace and holiness, truth and life, for these are the hallmarks of the kingdom of God" (No. 67).

letter carriers to keep our secular world going. We have still other people who serve Christ through his church: namely, us! Our public servants are the hierarchy: the bishops, priests, religious, and deacons of the church. Their vocation is to serve the entire church by teaching, guiding, and loving the people of God. We have not always thought of our hierarchy as "servants." But one of the titles by which the pope is known is *Servus servorum Dei*—the servant of the servants of God.

We all serve—minister—in different ways, each according to the gifts and talents God has given us. We serve as teachers, counselors, ministers of the Eucharist, ministers of the word. But ministry in the church goes beyond these few. People called to marriage minister by loving each other and doing all that is possible to keep the relationship growing and strong. Parents minister by extending their love to their children and taking charge of their spiritual, as well as physical, emotional and psychological growth. Single people minister by living lives filled with Christ and service to others.

With our human penchant for organization, we sometimes tend to think of the church in terms of the chain of command of the hierarchy: pope to cardinals, archbishops, bishops, priests, deacons, and "down" to the laity. But our spiritual organization is much more like a circle than a pyramid: Christ is at the center, and all of us—regardless of ministry—are joined in faith around him.

The Family Church

What better place to nurture our Christian vocation of love and service than within the loving arms of a Christian family? As an intimate community of love, the family dedicated to Christ becomes a church-community as well. Within this church, its members grow physically, emotionally, and spiritually. And it is from this loving growth that its members can then extend Christ's message into other communities and become missionaries of God's love to all people.

VATICAN II

"Every family, in that it is a society with its own basic rights, has the right freely to organize its own religious life in the home under the control of the parents" (Decree on Religious Liberty, No. 5).

The Sacraments: Christ Shares His Life With Us

We have already seen that the church is both divine and human, and that its purpose is to continue Christ's saving action in the world. Therefore, we are trying to express a divine reality in human terms. This would be an impossible task, had Christ not shown us the way. Christ is the perfect expression of our relationship with God.

Have you ever been forced to communicate in another language? When I was transferred to Cyprus, I went on ahead of my family to make living arrangements. This was my first experience of being a member of a minority group: the food was strange, the language was strange, and the customs were strange. So there I was, thousands of miles away from my roots in Illinois, trying to communicate with a Greek Cypriot on the rental price of a house. His English was minimal and my Greek non-existent, and his English got worse as I tried to tell him his price was too high. I was so frustrated that I even tried talking to him in Hebrew, a language I had studied in the Navy. I thought that since we were in the Middle East, maybe he would know the language, too. No such luck. He just thought my American accent was the strangest he had ever heard.

Eventually, however, we came to an agreement, and after a year in Cyprus, Sozos and his wife Nikki had become our good friends as well as landlords. We had learned a little Greek and their English took on a distinctly Midwestern accent.

What Sozos and I needed during our first attempts to communicate was an interpreter, someone who could understand both of us and help us understand each other. Christ, in a sense, is our interpreter. He translates the divine call of God into human terms, and helps us understand our Father.

The innocent questioning of a child may also require translation. As parents, we are always trying to explain adult ideas or situations in ways understandable to our children. "But, Mom, why can't I have a baby sister?" is not always easy to answer, is it? We could try to relate all the considerations that go into family planning but would they mean anything to a 5-year-old? Of course not. We have to answer the question in terms the child will understand.

So it is with the divine mystery. We humans are forced to express an unchangeable divine reality in terms which, because they are human, are constantly changing.

Sacraments are celebrations of our relationship with God. They are symbols expressed in human terms, which communicate God's loving call to us. They provide public, communal opportunities for each of us to encounter God, to consummate our covenant with God.

NCD

"Since the Christian family is a 'domestic Church,' prayer and worship are central to it. Christian family life involves prayerful celebration within the family, as well as liturgical celebration in the parish community of which it is an integral, active part" (No. 226).

In the pages that follow, we will talk about our sacraments. We will also talk about family forms of these sacraments which can serve to complement our formal celebrations in church. We ask you to bear in mind three things as you read:

1. Since sacraments are human expressions of divine reality, the outward signs of a sacrament can change without altering its divine purpose. The sacraments serve as encounters of divine love and power. Our external rituals themselves do not automatically cause God's power to flow like some magical on/off switch. Rather, the externals of the sacramental rite should help us be as receptive and as responsive as we can be to receive God. This is why we need not be afraid that all of the changes which have happened in the church over the last 20 years will destroy the church or the sacraments; rather, the church is adapting its external forms to express an inner reality in contemporary terms.

2. Sacraments are public celebrations of divine encounters. Part of our human language is ritual, in which we use signs and symbols to represent the reality which is taking place. The rituals are important only as long as they remain understood and understandable as symbols, not as ends in themselves.

We celebrate, through sacramental ritual, both sides of the encounter with God: both his call and our response. But just because the ritual is over doesn't mean the encounter is ended. Think about a little child who goes to communion but who is obviously distracted and whose mind is on something far away from an encounter with the Lord. Has she received Christ in the Eucharist? Of course. But she may not benefit fully from the encounter since the ritual of her response to God's call is not reflecting her true inner response. So, while a sacramental ritual may be complete, we must still carry our response forward into our lives.

3. Theologians today generally talk about sacraments in several different ways: they speak of Christ as the sacrament of encounter with God, the church as the sacrament of Christ, the seven sacraments of the church, and lastly, people or things which bring us to an encounter with God.

The Seven Sacraments

The church has seven special encounters with God, encounters which are important celebrations within the family of God. These celebrations mark the same occasions which bring any family together: birth, coming of age, making up after a fight, making life decisions, visiting sick friends, and gathering for those special family dinners. Through these sacraments, God shows us that he is with us in everything we do, say, think, or feel. Through the salvation of Jesus and the power of the Spirit, God laughs with us, cries with us, and loves with us.

The seven sacraments are grouped by their function within our faith-family: celebrations of *initiation* and growth in the family, celebrations of *healing* within the family, and celebrations of *commitment* to the family.

Initiation	Healing	Commitment
Baptism	Reconciliation	Holy Orders
Confirmation	Anointing of the Sick	Matrimony
Eucharist		

Sacraments of initiation

Through baptism, Christians are reborn; through confirmation, we are strengthened for further growth in Christ; through the Eucharist, we are fed.

1. *Baptism.* Baptism welcomes a person into God's family. It marks us as God's children, giving us his name, just as our human father gave us his name. Through the water, we are washed free of any sin, and with the oil we are dedicated to God. Baptism, like all the sacraments, is a celebration for the individual and the community. The newly-baptized celebrate their personal conversion, and the faith-family rejoices at the presence of God witnessed through the new Christians. The community and especially the parents are charged with supporting and helping the new Christians in continued growth toward God.

2. *Confirmation.* Confirmation renews and strengthens the Christian's call to bear witness to Christ. It celebrates the maturing of the Christian as he or she comes of age. The faith-family recognizes the challenge facing the mature man or woman of God, and celebrates the descent of the Spirit in his fullness to strengthen and inspire. Just as human life is taking on added responsibilities and greater depth, so will our relationship with Christ and one another. Celebrating events such as these within the family church as well as within the church family will confirm the young adult's awareness of God's continued presence and love within his or her life.

3. *Eucharist.* The Eucharist is the focal point of our lives, since all that belongs to Catholic Christian life "leads to the eucharistic celebration or flows from it. . . . The other mysteries (sacraments) dispose people to participate fruitfully in the central mystery of the Eucharist" (*NCD*, No. 120). By sharing in the real body and blood of Christ, we not only *re-enact* Christ's sacrifice, we *relive* it. Within the Eucharist we are united with our brothers and sisters in communion with our God and brother, Jesus Christ. In this world there can be no greater symbol of our intimate love relationship with God.

Sacraments of healing

We are brought into God's family by the sacraments of initiation. "When we have been weakened by sin or sickness, we are healed and strengthened within that body by the sacraments of Reconciliation and Anointing of the Sick" (*NCD,* No. 123).

NCD

"Everyone needs this sacrament, [reconciliation] for we are all sinners, not just those seriously estranged from God and the Church, and we all find here an opportunity to confront our sinfulness, acknowledge our need for conversion, seek pardon and peace and celebrate our union with the healing, merciful Christ and His Church" (No. 125).

4. *Reconciliation.* Jesus says: "The time has come and the kingdom of God is close at hand. Repent, and believe the Good News" (Mk 1:15). But Jesus realizes that this conversion away from sin and toward God is a constant, lifelong process. Along the way, we will be weakened by sin, which is a "willful rejection, either partial or total, of one's role as a child of God and a member of His people" (*NCD,* No. 98). Through the sacrament of reconciliation, God reaches out again to us, consoles us in our moment of failure and draws us back into him and our faith-family. Once again we celebrate God's forgiveness and power, and in the process the entire community is strengthened.

5. *Anointing of the Sick.* In administering this sacrament we used to emphasize ministry to the dying. But the gospels are full of examples of Christ's care and concern for the sick. So now we minister to all seriously ill persons who need its special comfort and support. Weakened in body, the sick are more susceptible to depression and fatigue of the spirit.

The church has always recognized the great gift of communal prayers for the sick.

> If one of you is ill, he should send for the elders of the church, and they must anoint him with oil in the name of the Lord and pray over him. The prayer of faith will save the sick man and the Lord will raise him up again; and if he

> has committed any sins, he will be forgiven. So confess your sins to one another, and pray for one another, and this will cure you; the heartfelt prayer of a good man works very powerfully (Jas 5:14-16).

Again, notice both the individual and communal aspects of the sacrament. God's saving power is accompanied by human love and support, so that the sick are "surrounded by the Church in the person of (their) family and friends" (*NCD*, No. 127).

Sacraments of commitment

As Christians, our membership in God's family calls us to serve that family. As a community, then, we join together to celebrate two forms of lifelong service—marriage and ordained ministry.

6. *Matrimony.* Matrimony celebrates the joyful expression of a man and woman's love for each other, and their dedication to nurture that love for the rest of their lives. It is a social contract. But even more, it is a covenant centered on Christ, and exemplifies the love of God for all people.

7. *Holy Orders.* The ordained ministry of priesthood consists of the orders of bishop, priest, and deacon. Each of these orders uniquely shares the service to the "priestly people" who make up our faith-community. "Let the greater among you be as the junior, the leader as the servant" (Lk 22:26). So, the priestly office is one of service; it is not authoritarian. No life of dedicated leadership is easy. Our ordained ministers are a part of our family and need our constant love, support, and encouragement. At ordination, a deacon, priest, or bishop receives God's sacred commission to care for the people of God through a life of service to the faith-community.

Family Sacraments

Human life celebrated with God becomes a sacrament in itself. As part of its prayer life, a family can and should celebrate special moments and events as complements to the sacraments we celebrate within the larger family of faith.

Family sacraments of initiation, such as celebrating a birthday or sharing a special family meal, can be effective symbols of God's action within the family. A family with a new baby can give thanks for the new life and the members can rededicate themselves to the family's growth and strengthening. And, as we saw in Chapter IV, when family meals are offered in Christ's name, they can be a form of eucharistic meal. The Eucharist and Mass take on deeper meaning when the family learns and lives out the *agape*—love-feast—at home.

The family can also celebrate the coming of age of its younger members as a form of confirmation. Celebrating this fact both within the family as well as within the larger community will confirm the young adult's awareness of God's continued active, loving presence within his or her life.

Sacraments of commitment may not lend themselves too easily to family applications. The coming marriage or ordination of a family member is appropriate for special family prayer and celebration, and an opportunity for the family to offer its intimate support for a member embarking on a lifelong journey. Promises and commitments made within the family for any variety of reasons are also opportunities to mirror the formal vows of the sacraments.

Probably no sacraments are more easily adaptable to family forms than the sacraments of healing. The need for reconciliation is lived out daily within families. Through countless little hurts and pettiness, we inflict pain and loneliness on the very people we want to love the most. What better way to reconcile than to first make up with the family member we have hurt and then celebrate it in the sacrament of reconciliation?

And if someone is sick, the family can come together and pray for God's blessing even before a priest arrives. While joining together like this to pray for a sick family member or friend may not always yield a dramatic and immediate healing, the social and spiritual benefits are incalculable.

We want to say again that these family forms are not meant to take the place of church sacraments; rather, they reflect the similar divine action which is taking place.

A FAMILY PENANCE

Recently, my family had made plans for a night out at a restaurant which had special entertainment for kids. We were all looking forward to it. But on the very day of the party, we learned that for several weeks Tommy had been giving his teachers fits by not doing his work, not concentrating in class and in general being a nuisance. That day he told his teachers he could not do his work for the next day because we were going to a "dinner party."

His behavior required immediate attention, and our special night out would be affected. If we kept Tommy home we would all miss out, but we agreed that this was the best way to work on the problem immediately and to show him how his actions had affected the rest of us.

When he came home, Tommy stoically

SCRIPTURE

"If you are bringing your offering to the altar and there remember that your brother has something against you, leave your offering there before the altar, go and be reconciled with your brother first, and then come back and present your offering" (Mt 5:23-24).

received his punishment, only part of which involved our dining out. In fact he was so stoic that I wondered if we'd been wrong about the impact that cancelling dinner would have. But then Stephen came home.

Steve's first question was "when do we leave for supper?" I had him ask his older brother what had happened. The confrontation between the two left no doubt in Tom's mind that his actions had hurt us all. The healing process began with this realization.

That night we celebrated what amounted to a healing service at our own table, letting Tom know that he was still loved. The impact was deep and his contrition real. Steve seemed a bit slow to forgive his brother, but he did by the time supper was over.

This whole experience helped Tom realize his responsibility to his family and helped show him that he needed to accept responsibility for his work at school. Several weeks later we received a call from school and were told that Tom's work was being done well and on time. Our family penance had turned into a family blessing.

A HEALING ACTION

My wife suffered from a severe form of hand eczema for 10 years. Her fingers and hands would become very rough and dry. They would crack open and bleed, even under the fingernails, causing her nails to fall off. The doctors at the local hospital told her there was no cure, but that they would try to relieve her discomfort. They put her on a strong medication and told her to keep her hands out of water. That was a little hard to do for a mother of three young children. Over a two-year period her medication was increased to the same level commonly prescribed for leprosy victims. Still, there was no improvement.

One Friday afternoon I came home to find her in extreme pain. Her fingers were swollen nearly twice normal size and so painful that she could not put them against anything. Each finger was encrusted with scabrous matter, pus, and blood. I immediately called the doctor who told me I could bring her in the next Monday or Tuesday. I told him she needed immediate help, and he told me—without seeing my wife or recalling the specifics of her condition—to double her medication, and that there was nothing more he could do until the following week.

I was at a loss. We had been working with this hospital for quite some time and with several dermatologists there. But the care being provided wasn't working.

After my wife passed a torturous night, I called some friends the next morning to ask for their prayers. Several hours later we were visiting some of the same friends and one casually suggested we go to a different clinic nearby. We contacted the clinic and my wife was seen quickly. The doctor examined her thoroughly and gave her an injection. He changed the medication and told us to come back in three days. Within 24 hours her hands had improved, and within 48 hours they looked almost normal—for the first time in many years. At her second visit the doctor reduced the medication and sent us on our way. Since then my wife's hands have been free of pain and as smooth as when we were dating. In short,

within a week a severe condition had been reversed and put under control.

In the joyful atmosphere which surrounded my wife's recovery, we reflected on the experience. We realized that God had answered our cries for help, and those of our friends. Secondly, we realized that God works through human agents. In this case, he worked through our friend who recommended the different clinic, and through the new doctor.

On a purely human level, I suppose our course of action was the only logical thing to do. But we had failed for years to comprehend that logic. We believe that God's healing action was giving us the vision to do what we did. My wife's hands have become a sign of God's direct power to heal all of us in the family.

To summarize our discussion of sacraments: We should develop a prayerful sense of the applicability of the seven sacraments of the church to our daily lives. Frequent participation in the sacraments should, of course, be encouraged for all family members since these sacraments are special opportunities to celebrate our faith in God's love. We should also develop a creative sense of the sacramental occasions present in the intimate context of family life. In this way Christ will become and remain the central figure in the family.

Ecumenism: Our Family Grows Together

Since Vatican II, large numbers of Christians of all denominations have been working hard for the reunion of all Christians.

> "I pray not only for these,
> but for those also
> who through their words will believe in me.
> May they all be one" (Jn 17:20-21).

The time is ending when we respond in fear and anger to the religious beliefs of others. This is not to say that we are forsaking our Catholic heritage or beliefs. Rather, we are now asked to look for the things we have in common with other churches: for example, a belief in God and Jesus Christ and the unifying action of the Spirit. Many of the differences between Catholic Christianity and Protestant Christianity have been blown out of proportion and we can help clear the air by our living witness to Christ, and by learning as much as we can about our faith so we can discuss it intelligently with others. As parents, we need to encourage this same process in our children, not out of fear, but so they can learn more deeply the far-reaching effects of Christ's prayer for unity. Such unity can only happen when fear is put aside and love put in its place.

SCRIPTURE

"And there are other sheep I have
that are not of this fold,
and these I have to lead as well.
They too will listen to my voice,
and there will be only one flock,
and one shepherd" (Jn 10:16).

VATICAN II

"The restoration of unity among all Christians is one of the principal concerns of the Second Vatican Council. Christ the Lord founded one Church and one Church only. . . . Everywhere large numbers have felt the impulse of this grace, and among our separated brethren also there increases from day to day a movement, fostered by the grace of the Holy Spirit, for the restoration of unity among all Christians" (Decree on Ecumenism, No. 1).

VI

RESPONDING IN LOVE

My children,
our love is not to be just words or mere talk,
but something real and active (1 Jn 3:18).

Love Is Serving

The call to love is God's message. It was given in the Old Testament to the Jews: "Love your neighbor as yourself" (Lv 19:18). And it was made real in Christ: "Love one another as I have loved you" (Jn 15:12). Since this love is based on an imitation of Christ it is a giving, healing, teaching, feeding, listening love. It is a love built of everyday life; a love of worn-out stories, dirty socks and the grind of a family's routine. It is the love of the people in our lives.

If we are to use Christ as an example of how to respond in love, we must accept service as the essence of love. To serve unconditionally is the model which Jesus lived, and the challenge which faces every Christian. And the call to service begins in the family. It begins with the creation of a sense of social responsibility and of the dignity of the individual. The family should convey this sense. Through day-to-day family experiences, values, attitudes and behaviors are conveyed to the child. Here the child develops a sense of self-worth and of the intrinsic dignity of people as an image of their

NCD

"The root cause of social injustice, selfishness and violence reside within the human person: the imbalances of the modern world are linked to a more basic imbalance in the human heart. Injustice, greed, lack of mercy, violence, and war are social consequences of sin" (No. 170).

creator. Once this respect for life and living is instilled, mercy, peace, and justice are natural reactions to the condition of individuals in need. If we are founded in a respect for the well-being of our neighbor, that person's poverty becomes intolerable. If we celebrate the gift of our life daily, the demeaning of another's life lessens us. This art of loving is learned from those who love us.

Planting the Seed of Love

Perhaps the most important function parents have in developing Christian love in their children is conveying an awareness of self-worth to them. Before children can love, forgive, take chances, enjoy and relate to others in more than purely selfish terms, they must have a sense of self-worth. This comes primarily from parents. It cannot be faked and is dependent on whether or not parents view them as loveable. Children will know if they are considered essentially an annoyance, something in the way of achieving other goals in life. But how do we, who love our children, nurture their self-dignity? We do it as Christ did for those he loved. We spend time with them; we talk to them; we share our visions and our fears, and most importantly, we accept them as they are. We must love our children as they are before we can exhort them to something we view as better. Jesus was a gentle teacher who always respected the dignity of those he instructed. When patiently describing his Father's kingdom with parable after parable, he used symbols and signs in nature. He was an effective rabbi (teacher) because he loved his students and he lived his message.

He accepts our level of understanding and meets us there. We have the same message to bring to our children: God loves us and wants us to love him back.

NCD

"Catechesis for justice, mercy, and peace is a continuing process which concerns every person and every age. It first occurs in the family by word and by example" (No. 170).

SCRIPTURE

"Above all, never let your love for each other grow insincere, since love covers over many a sin" *(1 Pt 4:8).*

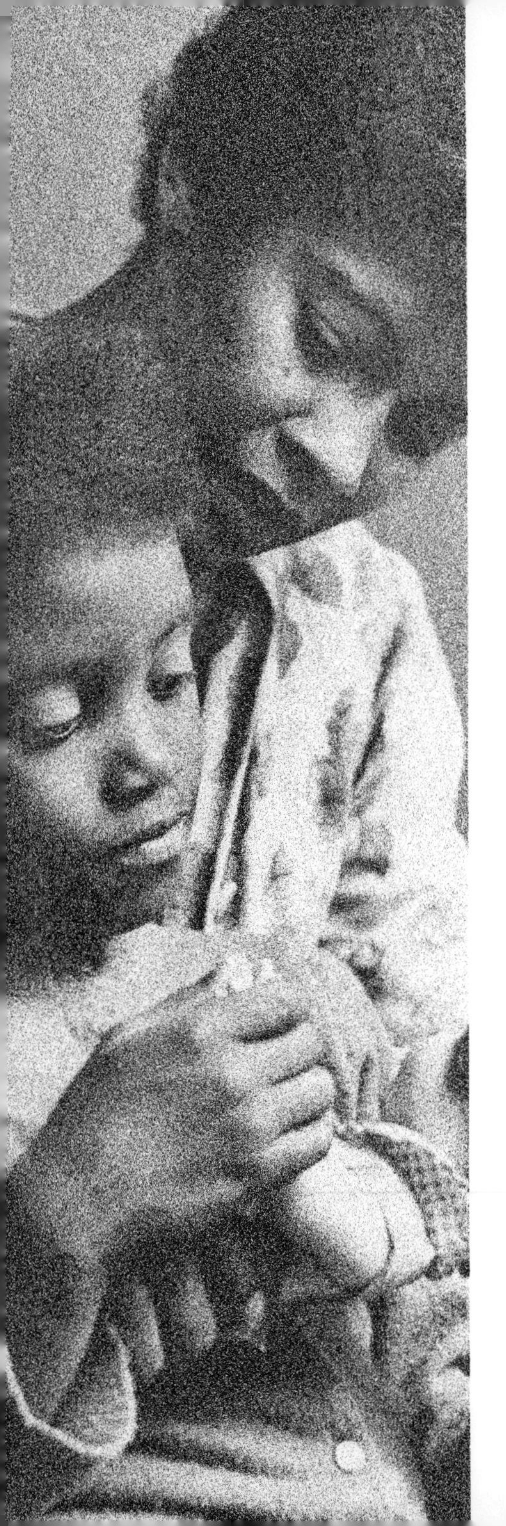

Nurturing Love

From fruits of virtue grows a tree of life (Prv 11:30).

The church defends and encourages our right as parents to be the primary educators of our children because we are the most influential human factor on their behavior. Our example is the model by which children will determine what is good, what is love. If we impose a set of standards on them that is not our own, we should expect eventual rebellion.

These dual standards can be very subtle. For example, most Catholics enroll their children in CCD or a parochial school to assist in their spiritual development, but how many of these parents have a program for their own spiritual growth? Can we demand that our children live a loving response to God, unless we try to do the same? This type of dual standard seems to be based on the hope that our children, by being force-fed at church and school, may take on a spirituality which really isn't our own. We teach our children how to love (or not love) more than our schools or churches do. For example, our family has discussed how we prepare for Mass, the love feast. However, what we *do* in preparation for the Eucharist is much more influential than what we *say* about it.

PREPARING FOR EUCHARIST

"Russ, you still haven't combed your hair, your room's a mess; get that old shirt off and get ready for Mass!"

"Is the new T-shirt OK?"

"No!"

"Why?"

"Because I said so."

"Where's my shoe?"

"Amy, if you put things where they belong you'd be able to find them. Where did you find the shoe you have?"

"In the laundry basket."

"Maybe the other shoe's there too. Now get going, we're late for Mass."

"Here it is in the bookcase."

"Don't forget the envelope!"

"I won't, and you don't have to remind me! Russ, you still aren't ready. Amy, for God's sake get that shoe on. That's it; I've had it; I'm leaving. You can come if you want."

In viewing this preparation, I found that my primary and maybe my only concern was getting to Mass on time. I didn't help the family get ready and in my impatience I was quick to condemn their lateness. Was our celebration of the Eucharist lessened by my inability to put my discomfort about being late aside and help my family? Did I love and did I teach love?

Our point is not that we should be so introspective or so self-critical that we accept total responsibility for our children's lives, for their ability or inability to love. We are their primary educators, but we do not take away their free will. We can be the most loving parents in the world, and still meet failure. With concern and the will to love with the strength of Jesus, we can help maximize our potential as parents.

Social Justice

If we have fostered love in our home, it is by our example of loving the people with whom we have con-

NCD

"The fundamental concept underlying the social teaching of the Church is the dignity of the person, a dignity rooted in likeness to God and the call to communion with Him" (No. 170).

"Catechesis strives to awaken a critical sense, leading to reflection on society and its values and to an assessment of the social structures and economic systems which shape human lives" (No. 170).

tact. But what about the neighbors we have never met, the starving masses, and the unknown refugees? Our church instructs us to love them as well. To be Christian, we must feel the pain of another's starvation and isolation and do what we can to lighten those burdens. It is difficult to love masses of people we do not know. However, our children often teach us that it is possible. Small children are amazingly compassionate when they are told stories of large-scale suffering, even though they may not understand the immensity of the numbers involved. This seems to be because they do not think in terms of starving masses or thousands of refugees. Instead, they relate to the image of a single starving child, or a homeless grandmother. Our children have described why they contributed to the missions, not in terms of the number of people who needed help but rather in terms of their compassion for an individual they picture. This, of course, is the lesson for us: The basis of social injustice is real individual suffering. We should be moved primarily by the image of a brother or sister in need as an image of Jesus.

Love and the Institution

Moved to what? To action, of course. What actions of ours can solve the world's problems? At this point we and our children are faced with the reality that social injustice may be beyond our individual ability to alleviate. We can then either choose apathy or a small role within a large social system. And so it is that the church urges us as individuals to support the institutions which are effecting social justice in the world. That love which was nurtured in the family, and which finds its daily expression in the one-on-one contacts of living, can thus expand to touch the world. The motivation stems from a sense of responsibility for our brothers and sisters.

We have to realize, however, that meeting our Christian responsibility through institutions poses some dangers. Institutions of all types are easy to give to because they give back. The church assures us of belonging to the followers of Christ. Charities can give us a sense of helping, without necessarily being involved. Our team gives us congratulations and trophies. But there are no trophies for parents, and if we fill our lives by giving to other institutions, we may not give enough time to our families. If we have to squeeze family into our lives, something's wrong. Institutions, especially those of the church, are excellent means of letting our love grow. But, in the long run our ability to support institutions is drawn from the love of the family, and the family must be nourished by the institution.

> In short, there are three things that last: faith, hope and love; and the greatest of these is love (1 Cor 13:13).

VATICAN II

"Among the various works of the family apostolate the following may be listed: adopting abandoned children, showing a loving welcome to strangers, helping with the running of schools, supporting adolescents with advice and help, assisting engaged couples to make a better preparation for marriage, taking a share in catechism-teaching, supporting married people and families in a material or moral crisis, and in the case of the aged not only providing them with what is indispensable but also procuring for them a fair share of the fruits of economic progress" (Decree on the Apostolate of Lay People, No. 11).

Saints—God's Heroic Lovers

We are all called to be saints. That's not just a figure of speech; it is a simple statement of fact. We are each called to be a "holy one"—a saint. Sainthood is determined by the strength of a person's response to God's love. The people we normally think of as saints have been publicly recognized by our faith community for the power of God which was shown through them and for their courageous and dedicated responses of love. They were not perfect beings, nor were they superhuman people above the cares, frustrations, and failures of day-to-day existence. In fact, some of them were originally among the world's greatest sinners. What set them apart was their eventual loving and active faith in God. These saints are shown to us by the church as heroic examples of the response which we

VATICAN II

"Today there is an inescapable duty to make ourselves the neighbor of every man, no matter who he is, and if we meet him, to come to his aid in a positive way" (Pastoral Constitution on the Church in the Modern World, No. 27).

SCRIPTURE

"I tell you solemnly, in so far as you did this to one of the least of these brothers of mine, you did it to me" (Mt 25:40).

are all called to live: the sainthood of the constantly-trying-forever-failing-and-trying-again people of God.

Studying the lives of the saints within the family really gives children and parents excellent role models. Personal sanctity can be viewed as something achievable and observable in our lives, not something certain people simply were born with.

ST. PETER AND JOSE

For many years, my favorite hero has been St. Peter—the rock. Peter is described in the Gospels as totally and delightfully human. Christ would praise him one minute and have to scold him the next. We already saw one of the best examples of this in Chapter II when Jesus asks the apostles who people think he is. Only Peter gives the right answer ("You are the Messiah") and Christ blesses him for being given this insight from God.

But immediately after, when Christ tells them that the messiah will have to suffer, Peter takes Jesus aside and argues with him, drawing a severe rebuke from Christ. How easy it is to identify with Peter, riding high after being praised by Christ in front of the rest of the twelve, so high that he feels confident enough to confront Christ. The result is that only seconds after "Blessed are you, Simon," is spoken, Christ turns and says, "Get out of my sight, you Satan!" In the Garden of Gethsemane, Peter alone *acts*; he draws his sword and strikes out at the armed guards surrounding Christ. It is the act of an impetuous yet courageous man who is willing to risk his own life without hesitation for a friend in danger. And yet,

only hours later, Peter's courage fails him and he denies repeatedly that he even knows Jesus.

Peter was a normal human being caught up in an extraordinary encounter with God. When we watch a movie or TV show in which the hero storms the beach, or single-handedly breaks up a vicious crime syndicate, we can take such courage for granted and see ourselves doing the same feats. But then, when facing a challenge not nearly so risky, like sticking up for a person we see being ridiculed or mistreated at work, we find we're not so courageous after all. It's easy to fall into this same trap when reading about the saints. *We* would never deny Christ; *we* would never contradict Christ.

What sets Peter apart from Judas? Both men were special friends of Jesus who ultimately denied and betrayed him. One big difference is that Peter remembered after his sin that Jesus still loved him and would forgive him. Judas despaired. Peter picks himself up and charges forward again, thanks to his courageous willingness to return to Christ in love. That is why we honor Peter: not because he didn't fall, but because of his ability to bounce back stronger than ever, using the strength that his faith in God gave him.

I have a friend who is a saint in the mold of Peter. Joseph came to his apostolate from a life of hard knocks and rough living. He responded to God's call in his late 20s, after he thought he had "done it all." He entered the seminary and was ordained a priest. Joseph found, as all priests must, that the imposition of a bishop's hands does not remove human weakness. Joseph tried

many ministries within the priesthood, but found his true calling in working with Mexican farm workers in the southwestern United States and California.

Joseph became known simply as "Padre Jose" by his friends. His ministry is marked by his humanness, his honest warmth and joy at being with people in all of their experiences. His own early life provides him with rare compassion and understanding of the human struggle of every person, and his witness to Christ's life in him is apparent by the way he lives his life and tells his story; he is a man who constantly needs and asks for God's help. He throws himself courageously into whatever action is needed to care for his friends, whether it be the formation of a new Christian community, or the elimination of a civil or social burden inflicted on the people. He is always aware of his own daily temptations and failures. In fact, Jose says he wouldn't think of getting out of bed in the morning until he has asked the Spirit to be with him to help him during the day. Jose is 67 now (although his joy makes him look much younger), and a living saint, a man who falls and rises again in the loving name of Jesus his Lord.

ST. FRANCIS AND RICHARD

St. Francis of Assisi is certainly one of the greatest figures of the church. His personal sanctity, and the effect he has had on the church for centuries were primarily due to his simple uncompromising following of the gospel. His gentleness, compassion and zeal have been a model of Christian life. His personal pentecost came in his mid-20s and led him to a life of Christlike service. Although humble and reserved he had a remarkable record as an evangelist, including preaching to Moslems during the crusades. His love of all God's creation is beautifully expressed in his writings, which have become classics of our own faith.

I always thought that St. Francis was too good to be true, bigger than life. I thought that the spirit of Francis was more an ideal than a real possibility for anyone to live by today. But then we met that spirit in Richard.

Richard was a sailor who was between ships, and temporarily without a home. We invited him into our house thinking we were his benefactors, and God's reward was Richard himself. God showed us through this saint that gentleness and compassion are as attainable for us as they were for Francis. While we were *working* at charity, Richard exuded it as a part of his nature. Richard was soft-spoken, thoughtful, and intoxicated with Jesus. He was a daily reminder that the Gospel is meant to be lived. Richard is not superhuman, but he was the closest example of what it means to live the fullness of the Gospel which we had ever met. Like Francis, Richard takes his spirituality into the secular world. His shipmates, the patients he treats as a Navy corpsman, and his military supervisors are as affected by his gentle yet powerful love as we are.

The Only Response: Love

A friend once said that everything we ever do in life is in reality an act of love: love of ourselves, love of God, love of others. Our constant struggle as Christians is to place the love of God and one another ahead of our self-love. God, our loving father, calls us to love him. In loving God, we find in Christ that we can tangibly express that love relationship—our new covenant—through our love for one another. "Anyone who loves God must also love his brother" (1 Jn 4:21). As parents, we are called to form and nourish the covenant within our families. In binding our lives together in the love of God, we mothers, fathers and children are real witnesses (saints) to the power of God's great love in the world. God is the center of our lives and is in our midst as a family. St. John tells us:

> God is love
> and anyone who lives in love lives in God,
> and God lives in him (1 Jn 4:16).

In ending, we would like to pray with you in the words of St. Paul:

> This, then, is what I pray, kneeling before the Father, from whom every family, whether spiritual or natural, takes its name:
>
> Out of his infinite glory, may he give you the power through his Spirit for your hidden self to grow strong, so that Christ may live in your hearts through faith, and then, planted in love and built on love, you will with all the saints have strength to grasp the breadth and the length, the height and the depth; until, knowing the love of Christ, which is beyond all knowledge, you are filled with the utter fullness of God (Eph 3:14-19).

A Parents' Litany

When the children have worn us out,
Out-questioned us,
Confused us,
Misbehaved
And left us a bundle of raw nerves,

Come Holy Spirit.

When the actions and motivations of
our children
Seem to equate to no more than
human selfishness,

Come Holy Spirit.

When our reason tells us we are only
social animals
And raising children is only
psychology and nutrition,

Come Holy Spirit.

We believe that our actions as
Christian parents can make a difference,
We believe we are the instruments of God
and that by remaining open to his Spirit,
we will be inspired to nurture our children

Come Holy Spirit.

Give us understanding to guide,
Patience to listen,
Strength to forgive
Give us the joy of loving children.
We believe,
And because we believe, we love.